SEX

POLITICS

RELIGION

How Delusional Thinking Is Destroying America

STEVE SIEBOLD

SEX POLITICS RELIGION

HOW DELUSIONAL THINKING IS DESTROYING AMERICA

Steve Siebold

Published by London House

ISBN: 978-0-9755003-8-5

DEDICATION

This book is dedicated to my Dad.

The most honest man I've ever known.

Walter C. Siebold, Jr.

1926-2011

ACKNOWLEDGMENTS

Dawn Andrews, my wife and best friend. You are the love of my life.

Bruce Serbin, my publicist. You are the best in the business.

Sandra Larson, our graphic designer and book cover specialist.

Brenda Robinson, my editor.

Charlie Fischer, my research assistant.

Thanks to everyone for all your help and support during this two year odyssey. I couldn't have done it without you.

INTRODUCTION

This may rank among the most controversial books ever written, but it shouldn't. The premise is simple, straightforward and brutally honest: Delusional thinking is destroying America and only critical thinking can save it. Here's what I mean: Delusional thinking is driven by emotion and defined by irrational conclusions. America is a great nation. I love this country. Our society and standard of living is the envy of the world. The problem is our population has become an army of drones, unwilling to think independently. Whether it's teachers, politicians, or religious leaders, everyone seems to be telling us what to think and how to live. And it has to stop in order for America to survive. It's time for us to wake up and realize that none of these people are any smarter than us. None are morally superior nor can they prove their way is the right way. It's time to take control of our own lives and start thinking for ourselves. Does the government really have the right to send an 18-year-old to war but deny him the right to drink? Should the pharmaceutical industry be demonized and scorned for being successful? Should religious ideals carry so much influence in government when the premise of their argument can't be proven? Shouldn't American citizens have the freedom to live their lives without limits as long as they're not hurting anyone else or infringing on others' rights? In a lifetime that lasts approximately 80 years, is there any reason we should waste a single minute being bullied by power hungry leaders and religious zealots who wish to control and manipulate us? These and many other of the biggest social issues of our time are debated in this book. The purpose is not to persuade you to adopt my ideology, but to motivate you to use critical thinking to draw your own conclusions. This requires a well-rounded education in the important areas of life, minus emotion and preconceived ideas. The only way to save America is to ask all Americans to save themselves, the foundational method of which is independent thought. Don't just accept what you're told. Educate yourself enough to push back and punch holes into outdated rituals, dogma and behaviors. If you do your homework, engage in emotionless critical thought and end up agreeing with your mentor, congressmen or minister, then adopt that belief with the condition that you will alter it if new contradictory evidence becomes available.

I hope this book doesn't offend you, but if it does, check the root of your indignation. Chances are you're reacting emotionally to an opposing idea that has triggered a deeply embedded fear in your consciousness that threatens the way you make sense of the world. Being offended by an opposing opinion is a classic example of emotionally driven irrational thought. If this occurs as you're reading this book, compartmentalize your emotions and move into critical thinking, where you'll reach the only logical conclusion in this equation: my world view is the opinion of one man, one person. One fallible human being who's no smarter than anyone else. Your opinions and ideas are equally important. I can only offer you mine and hope someday to hear yours. Together we are more intelligent than we are individually.

As you read this book, you might wonder why I wrote it, and you won't be the first to ask. Most of my friends and colleagues thought the same thing. The reason is simple: I love America and I want us to prosper. The problem is when it comes to discussing the critical social issues of the 21st century, we have the collective emotional maturity of an adolescent. We adamantly and sometimes viciously defend beliefs and philosophies that were conceived during the Dark Ages. The only reason we have been able to operate so successfully under this emotionally stunted cloud is due to our great wealth and power. It's time for America to grow up emotionally, shed the dogma of our puritanical roots, and take our place among the most socially evolved nations in the world. It will take a psychological revolution to make this happen, and I hope this book will serve as a catalyst for the movement.

Sex, Politics and Religion: How Delusional Thinking is Destroying America is about applying critical thinking to our country's most pressing problems. I define critical thinking in its most basic form, which is reaching conclusions based on greater criteria devoid of emotion. This level of thought goes far beyond positive and wishful thinking, which many American's mistakenly believe to be the holy grail of consciousness.

The key to becoming a critical thinker is mental toughness, which is the ability to control and manipulate your emotions. Until enough American's get mentally tough enough to approach our problems through emotionless critical thought, we are destined to repeat the mistakes of the past. I'm confident we can make it happen.

Thank you for the opportunity to offer my thoughts and ideas for your consideration. I look forward to hearing yours.

Steve Siebold

June 1, 2012

TABLE OF CONTENTS

SEX 1

SEX

SEX IN AMERICA

The human sex drive is the most powerful force on earth. Harnessed and celebrated, it's a beautiful, natural phenomenon that produces unparalleled pleasure. People have risked fame, fortune, and their very lives in pursuit of the ultimate sexual experience. Yet in America, we learn little about sex as children and are brainwashed to believe it's wrong unless we are married. Our culture of sexual repression makes America appear naive and immature in relation to many parts of the world. The delusional thinking around sex in America is derived primarily from puritanical dogma that bullies us into believing sex is a sin. Critical thinking says nothing will ever stop the most primal drive that smolders within the human psyche. Nature will always favor this form of expression, no matter how many fanatics threaten us with eternal damnation. Religious and political leaders in America are notorious for delivering speeches and sermons with puritanical fervor, while simultaneously engaging in the same acts they condemn. Whether it's the President of the United States or the hellfire evangelical, the hypocrisy among American leaders is legendary. And sex scandals are not new to America. From Ben Franklin to Thomas

Jefferson, senators and congressmen, to hundreds of Catholic priests—all have participated in what many describe as sexual misconduct. Sex is an undeniable force that can manifest itself positively or negatively, but make no mistake: it will manifest itself. The Catholic Church has taken centuries to learn this lesson through its mandate of celibacy in the priesthood, which has been the foundation for 2,000 years of child rape and every other conceivable form of sexual abuse.

Until America grows up emotionally and embraces the idea that sex among consenting adults is to be celebrated, we will be at the mercy of the hypocrites behind the pulpit and in Washington. Guilt, shame, and fear have always been the weapons of choice for the self-righteous, and they wield them on the masses to coerce conformity to their moral standards. It's hard to blame people who lived during the Dark Ages for not applying their brain power or using their critical thinking skills, but in the 21st century it's just embarrassing. When 300 million smart, educated people are willing to psychologically submit to a self-serving government and corrupt religious code plagued by scandal, financial malfeasants, and abuse, something is wrong.

The solution is critical thinking, which celebrates sex, releases people from the guilt of engaging in it consensually, and educates us on how to safely enjoy it. What Americans do without infringing on the rights of others should be up to them. Whether they are straight, gay, transgender, or any other orientation, they should be respected and left alone. The only area where the government should engage is in comprehensive sex education in the public school system. The citizens of the richest country in the world learn about sex on the streets. Our outdated school system refuses to adequately educate our children on how to harness and safely navigate the most powerful force in nature. We spend our entire lives guessing how to be sexually successful when excellent information could be built into our school curriculum. The root of the problem is religious dogma and the leaders who perpetuate it. Until we either update these archaic sexual beliefs or ditch them altogether, we will continue to suffer the consequences of conscious and purposeful ignorance. The problem is, our political and spiritual leaders are either living in the past or are terrified to evolve. Running for office on the platform of sexual evolution will not get you elected. The religious zealots will happily and viciously destroy any chance you might have of helping this country grow up. This is why we have right-wing funded robots in Washington who refuse to answer questions in a straightforward manner. The fact is America must evolve or die. In this first section, I'm going to make my case for social evolution in areas related to sex. Some may consider my ideas to be radical and unrealistic in a country dominated by organized religion, but you will notice a common thread that runs through each argument: personal choice and self-government. If it's not hurting someone else, government should stay out of it. After all, who are bureaucrats to tell us how to live? As I stated in the introduction, I'm in no way attempting to convert you to living your life in a certain way. All I am fighting for is for all of us to be able to make our own choices and live life on our own terms, minus interference from church or state. If critical thinking tells you to follow Jesus Christ, Buddha, or Scientology, I believe you should have the freedom to do so. But when your beliefs start infringing on my freedom, something needs to be done, and that's exactly what's happening in America. I hope this book will help stimulate the national conversation in a peaceful, respectful, non-threatening way where we can all have a voice. After all, isn't that what America is all about?

TRADITIONAL MARRIAGE

I like being married. I've been married to my best friend for almost 30 years, and our relationship is the cornerstone of my life. But statistically speaking, marriage as an institution is a failure. We all know the figures, but in case you've been in a coma, here they are: about 50% of married couples get divorced, and of the couples who stay married, a good percentage have affairs, are unhappy, or stay married for money or children. When choices are limited to survival, freedom and fearless thinking are a luxury. The woman who marries because she's pregnant and penniless is happy to have a roof over her head and a man by her side. Who can blame her? It's easy to criticize, but if you've ever been broke, scared and lonely, any alternative is attractive. But for most of us this isn't the case. In America, we marry for love and companionship, which are good reasons. The problem is it only works well for a small percentage of people, because half get divorced and an additional percentage of the couples who stay married are unhappy. Marriage remains popular due to societal pressure and religious programming. It's promoted as the foundation of American society, and if this were actually true, America would be an abysmal failure.

The foundation of America is freedom, not marriage. But religious leaders want us to believe its marriage because it's a religious practice that gives them more control over the populous. The delusional thinking around marriage is that one person has the ability to fulfill all of our physical, emotional, and spiritual needs for a lifetime. This is a weak, unsustainable premise. I mean, really, who on earth is magnificently multidimensional enough to fulfill another person's every need, wish, and desire? This is the primary reason marriage fails and is not the cornerstone of society. Americans have always challenged conventional thinking, and that one habit has made us rich and powerful. When it comes to marriage, most people abandon independent thinking and allow themselves to be coerced into compliance. Societal brainwashing and emotional drunkenness are substituted for critical thinking, and this is where the problems begin. Sexual attraction and the giddiness of love subside, and everyday life takes over. Best case scenario is you picked someone with a value system you both respect. Worst case is you didn't, and you're stuck with someone you don't even like. Either way, critical thinking says relying on one person to fulfill all of your needs for life is a recipe for disaster, and the results prove it. If marriage is ever going to reach its full potential, it needs to be updated. For those who are happily succeeding, no modifications are necessary. The good news is there are large and small subgroups around the country that have successfully altered their marriage contract to fit their particular needs and enrich their relationships. These groups include, but are not limited to, God-Centered Marriage, Open Marriage, The Lifestyle, and Polyamory. These are just a few of the most popular maverick subgroups, but the couples who practice them number in the millions. If any of these marriage strategies seem offensive, I challenge you to open your mind and give them ample consideration. You may be exposed to a life-changing alternative. Before you pass judgment on these marital trailblazers, allow me to pose a Critical Thinking Question:

If you say you're satisfied with your marriage, are you really satisfied or are you unsure of how or afraid to make the changes that would make it outstanding?

This question may irritate or infuriate you, and I'll ask you to compartmentalize your anger in order to ensure critical thinking. Emotions cloud judgment, and this is one of the most important questions you'll ever answer: Is there anything you would change about your relationship that would make it more fulfilling, exciting or fun? Does your partner really satisfy every need you have, from intellectual, emotional, and sexual stimulation to having common interests, philosophies and goals? Please don't answer right away, and if you already did, make it a tentative answer and sleep on it. My only goal is to motivate you to dissect this life-changing question. The good news is, no matter what conclusion you reach, there is a solution. And if you decide that your marriage is perfect and can't be improved, you have no problem. And maybe before I go any further, let me respond to those of you who are saying, "Grow up, Siebold. Marriage is not just about sex, stimulation and excitement. It's about raising a family and taking care of one another." I agree, but...what if you could have it all? Maybe you can't imagine a marriage firing on all cylinders. I understand this is beyond many people's belief systems; but that doesn't mean it isn't possible. Millions of couples are already experiencing it. If you're not living your life like it's a short bold adventure, you're missing out. Because no matter how seriously you take it or how many risks you avoid, you will eventually run out of time.

If you're still reading by this point there's still hope for you. Most people shut down when they hear opposing ideas and philosophies. Questioning the way someone makes sense of the world invokes terror. After all, what if everything we've believed about life and living is wrong?

If you conclude that you don't have a perfect marriage, let's explore your critical thinking options.

Option One: Settle and be grateful for what you have. Many psychologists say this is your best hope for happiness. History proves that human beings are capable of happiness under even the most dire of circumstances. The critical thinking question is—why would you settle for mediocrity if you have a choice? If this is what you choose, I challenge you to look at life from 10,000 feet. The end of your life is getting closer with every breath. This is not fatalistic philosophy but unalterable objective reality. When you remove emotion from the equation you see life as it instead of what you wish it was. Delusion creates confusion, and a confused mind is incapable of living an optimal life. It's smart to be grateful because it fosters feelings of fulfillment, but settling when you have a choice is emotional cowardice.

Option Two: Get a divorce. In some cases this is the only answer, and other times it's the easy way out. The perfect mate doesn't exist. We all have our idiosyncrasies, annoying habits, and personality flaws. When you dump one mate for another all you're doing is trading one set of things you like and dislike for another set of things you like and dislike. Sometimes the differences matter, other times it's an even exchange. Marriage partners have upsides and downsides. Before you decide to get divorced make sure that you're not ditching one set of problems for another, and any marriage counselor will tell you this happens every day.

Option Three: Endure an unhappy marriage. This is not worth considering unless you have no choice. I would love to take the side of my motivational speaker friends who say we always have a choice, but that's not always true. Life is not a black and white, zero-sum game. It's tinted with shades of grey and middle ground, and sometimes that means choices are limited or non-existent. That being said, most of us do have a choice, and choosing to endure an unhappy marriage, even for the sake of children, is unwise. In the interest of full disclosure, I don't have children, and that may skew my ideology. But I would argue from unemotional thinking that children suffer more from the tension and nastiness of being raised by parents who despise one another than they do when parents get divorced. I've known dozens of couples who lack respect for one another and their kids know it. Children are smart and they sense mutual contempt a mile away.

Option Four: Have an affair. This requires the complete abandonment of critical thinking. According to relationship expert and infidelity counselor Suzie Johnson, from www.goasksuzie.com, the number one reason people have affairs is boredom. "Boredom is the kryptonite of marriage," says Johnson. "Men cheat because they don't believe they can honestly get what they want in their marriage. Women cheat because they feel deprived of romance. It's not the sex that's so destructive, but the deceit." The number of married people who have affairs is difficult to estimate, but some experts claim that 35-45% of spouses are cheating. The illicit affair is the worst solution since it's rooted in deception, and the potential damage is huge. It's a multidimensional betrayal of the heart, mind, and soul, and critical thinking says to avoid it at all costs.

Option Five: Modify your marriage. This is probably the best option of all if you have the guts to challenge societal norms and conventional wisdom. Millions of married couples are quietly creating their own rules for marriage, knowing if they are discovered by others they will be discriminated against, ridiculed, and punished by family, friends, employers, and society in general. America has a long and ongoing history of discrimination and moral judgment. The religious extremists hiding behind the cloak of Christianity are among the most vicious viola-tors. This is why many couples who modify their marriage refuse to reveal the inner workings of their success. Until America matures, these people will continue to flourish in secret societies, hiding some highly intelligent strategies for creating a world-class marriage. There are many more of these groups than I can document in this book, but next are a few of the most successful.

"Millions of married couples are quietly creating their own rules for marriage, knowing if they are discovered by others they will be discriminated against, ridiculed, and punished by family, friends, employers, and society in general."

CRITICAL THINKING QUESTION

Do you have the intellectual capacity and emotional maturity to openly challenge the practical limitations and social expectations of traditional marriage?

RECOMMENDED RESOURCE

Marriage Confidential: The Post-Romantic Age of Workhorse Wives, Royal Children, Undersexed Spouses & Rebel Couples Who Are Rewriting The Rules, by Pamela Haag

GOD-CENTERED MARRIAGE

These extremely religious couples hold their belief in God above everything else in their life. Many of them attend church multiple times per week and fellow congregants are the nucleus of their social lives. They come from various faiths and worship different gods. It's not what church they attend, religion they follow, or god they worship, that makes the difference, but the level of cohesiveness their focus creates as a couple. The supernatural aspect of God-Centered Marriage makes it unlike any other marriage that has a central focus, such as children, hobbies, or sports. The God-Centered Marriage works not only through a common focus and shared belief system, but it also offers the inherent advantage of the joint belief between the couple that any problem they encounter is either meant to be or will be handled by God. Unresolved disputes, character flaws, and other misfortunes are immediately prayed about and turned over to God, and if no resolution occurs, the couple believes that it's God's will. The unfaltering belief in the all-knowing, all powerful deity creates answers to all questions, and the unresolved are chalked up to being beyond human comprehension yet completely understood by God. "We go to God first for all of our decisions," says Christy Hey, who along with Justin, her husband of eight years, practices God-Centered Marriage. "And almost all of our friends have a God-Centered Marriage". Jay Travis, who's been married to Stephanie for five years, says "This is a great strategy for the faithful. The problem with marriage is that it's treated like dating. American society is devolving. An example is people living together." Travis goes on to say that the key to a successful marriage is "looking inside yourself for issues and superior communication with your spouse." God-Centered Marriage may be extreme, but it seems to work for the faithful who embrace it. The delusion is that the essence of its success is supernatural, or beyond having a common focus and belief system. In a country boasting a 50% divorce rate, the idea that God is guiding couples is questionable. Critical thinking says that whatever the catalyst of their success, followers of God-Centered Marriage are happily succeeding while not infringing on anyone else.

"In a country boasting a 50% divorce rate, the idea that God is guiding couples is questionable. Critical thinking says that whatever the catalyst of their success, followers of God-Centered Marriage are happily succeeding while not infringing on anyone else."

CRITICAL THINKING QUESTION

If God is guiding couples through marriage, why are so many people divorced or unhappy?

RECOMMENDED RESOURCE

Simple Secrets Couples Should Know: Enjoying a God-Centered Marriage, by Bob Barnes and Emilie Barnes

OPEN MARRIAGE

These couples allow one another to seek and maintain romantic relationships outside their marriage. Some advocates refer to this as "free market marriage" that invites competition and brings out the best in everyone. Detractors call it immoral. I interviewed 10 couples who have an open marriage for this chapter. Out of those 10, 7 rated themselves extremely satisfied with open marriage; 2 were satisfied and 1 was getting divorced. The 70 % of couples who said they were extremely satisfied used words like "excitement" and "thrill." According to multiple sources, America boasts approximately 30 million couples involved in some form of open marriage. Unfortunately, due to America's emotional immaturity, most of these couples are thriving in secret for fear of discrimination. This is sad, because of all the couples I interviewed, not one was attempting to promote this lifestyle to anyone else. They simply wish to be free to live their lives, yet almost all of them said they look forward to the day when they no longer have to lie to friends and family about their relationship, especially since they are so happy with their results. "I come from a southern Baptist family, and if they knew my wife and I had an open marriage, they would disown me and tell me I was going to hell," said one man. "They simply don't have the emotional capacity to handle it." Another couple, in their late 50s said, "My husband and I have been married for 32 years and we've had an open relationship almost from the beginning. We've had many beautiful, loving, romantic relationships with other people over the years, and it's created an unbreakable bond between us. I know it sounds counterintuitive, but we have 30+ years of evidence to prove it." The couples I interviewed were difficult to find and would only agree to speak with me if they remained anonymous. Once we established trust, they were more than willing to share their stories. One of the biggest surprises was a newly-wed couple from Wisconsin who are both 25-years-old and had already agreed to have an open marriage before they walked down the aisle. "You might wonder why we even got married. The truth is we are crazy in love and wanted to make a commitment to one another," the newly minted husband confessed. "We were both raised outside Milwaukee by strong Catholic families and became disillusioned with all the fear-based manipulative doctrines of the church. When it comes to our relationship, we're making the rules, and that means partnership not ownership." Pretty impressive philosophy for 25-year-olds. I found it interesting that both of them had recently graduated from Yale University and appeared to be exceptionally intelligent. According to several relationship experts

I interviewed, there seems to be a significant correlation between high-level education, above average intelligence, and couples who seek open and other non-traditional relationships, and it seems to be even more prevalent in the new generation of 20-somethings. "These kids are too educated and intelligent to buy into the religious, political, and societal dogmas of the past," said one academic advisor at an Ivy League university. "They're living life on their terms and making the rules as they go." And as you'd expect, the puritanical establishment is none too happy about it. Radio personality Dr. Laura Schlessinger told her listeners last year, "Most of our young people have absolutely no concept of morality." Columnist David Brooks wrote in the New York Times that "It's depressing how bad young people are at thinking and talking about moral issues." The question I have for Dr. Schlessinger and Mr. Brooks is, "Whose moral code are you referring to?" Their comments imply that an objective moral code has been previously established and agreed upon by society. It has not. I'm quite sure that many people find open marriage immoral. Organized religion is so ingrained in our collective consciousness it's amazing anyone can escape its manipulative spell. The younger generation isn't immoral, they are simply thinking for themselves. This is a skill most people have turned over to their boss, spouse, or minister. Dr. Deborah Anapol, a San Francisco based clinical psychologist and one of the world's foremost experts on the open relationship says, "America is a culture of openness and honesty, which is what open marriage is all about. The problem is, the majority of people lack the emotional intelligence to handle an open relationship." Open marriage is certainly not for everyone, but for the millions of couples who have the emotional savvy and motivation to navigate it, it's a successful solution. And with nearly 10% of the American population engaged in one form of it or another, it's clearly working for many couples. "Open marriage is growing in popularity and will continue to grow," claims Dr. Anapol. I believe she's right. The never-ending newness and the intellectual, emotional, and sexual variety of dating and mating with different partners are too attractive to fade away. Contrasted with traditional marriage it seems like an intelligent alternative for couples who embrace it. On the downside, the couples I spoke to suggested that I warn people of the risks involved in this lifestyle selection. "If your marriage isn't rock solid, don't even think about engaging in an open lifestyle," said a 32-year-old mother of 3. "If you're not in a mature, respectful, and happy marriage you are playing with fire. This is not a fix for a bad marriage." After I pushed for details on this comment, she continued: "It's not the outside partners that break up an open marriage; it's the married partners who destroy it from within because of their inability to cope with their own fear and jealousy. If you need to own and possess your spouse, open marriage is not for you." The delusional thinking around open marriage is that it's morally wrong. Marriage and monogamy are both cultural failures for a reason: they work against human nature and in many cases breed apathy, boredom, and resentment. Critical thinking says that social, cultural, and sexual variety offer us a richer, deeper and spiritually superior quality of life than the stagnation many couples experience. Traditional marriage vs. open marriage is essentially a stagnant relationship vs. a dynamic relationship. It's certainly not for every couple, especially the jealous or faint of heart, but its success is noteworthy and worth consideration. With their numbers growing well into the millions, there's little doubt we'll be hearing more from this underground movement in the future.

"America is a culture of openness and honesty, which is what open marriage is all about. The problem is the majority of people lack the emotional intelligence to handle an open relationship." — Dr. Deborah Anapol

CRITICAL THINKING QUESTION

Do you have the emotional intelligence to successfully navigate the jealousy and stressors that may arise in an open marriage?

RECOMMENDED RESOURCE

Opening Up: A Guide to Creating and Sustaining Open Relationships, by Tristan Taormino

THE LIFESTYLE

This marriage modification began in the early 1970s at the height of the sexual revolution in the form of key parties, where couples would throw a party and toss their keys into a bowl. At the end of the evening the guests would pick a key from the bowl, and whomever it belonged to was their sex partner for the night. Later on, this activity became known as wife swapping, and eventually evolved into 'swingers'. By the 1990s there were millions of couples attending parties, joining private clubs, and meeting other couples online. As a strategy to increase discretion, people started calling this "The Lifestyle." When couples were introduced in a traditional environment and suspected the other might be swingers, they would test them by asking, "Are you in the Lifestyle?" Couples that were could be identified immediately, and couples that were not had no idea what the term meant. There are approximately 5-7 million couples in the Lifestyle in America, although some experts say the number is much higher. No one knows for sure since few people in the movement can afford to reveal their identity. The Lifestyle is still underground but is growing so fast that Oprah Winfrey, 60 Minutes, and other national television shows have done major stories on it. I've interviewed couples from across America who are involved, and the number one benefit they cite is the positive impact the Lifestyle's lifestyle has had on their marriage. Don and Katherine are a middle aged couple from Palm Beach, Florida, who have been involved in the Lifestyle for the past eight years. Don says, "It's enhanced our relationship significantly. We love each other more than ever and our sex life is on fire." Katherine adds, "The sex with other people is exciting, but the real heat happens when we get back together. It's like throwing gas on a fire." This was the most common thing I heard from the couples I interviewed. When I visited swing clubs and met with the owners, they said that most of the members come to the club to flirt and dance, but 80% never engage other couples for sex. One woman at the Trapeze Club in Ft. Lauderdale said: "We've been members of this club for years, and the main reason is we love the atmosphere. It's a sexually charged, uninhibited, fearless environment where anything goes and no means no. I've never felt so sexy and safe at the same time."

The series Oprah Winfrey did on the Lifestyle revealed the same types of positive commentary. Couples in the Lifestyle are respectable people living their own way with no apologies and they don't push their philosophy on anyone else. Rita, a sixth grade school teacher from Dallas, has been in the Lifestyle for 23 years and said:

"People in the Lifestyle come from all walks of life. They're policeman, lawyers, doctors, plumbers, and so on. They are ordinary people with extraordinary sex lives. Most of my closest friends are in the Lifestyle." The delusional thinking around the Lifestyle is that it's all about sex. Sex is a part of the Lifestyle, but critical thinking says what it's really about is the feeling of freedom and cultivation of friendships with people who are sexually liberated enough to live life on their own terms. These people are on the leading edge of the post-sexual revolution and having a blast. It's not for everyone, and the couples involved will be the first to tell you so. "If you can't handle seeing your partner being kissed and caressed by another person, the Lifestyle is not for you. If you're possessive, paranoid or jealous, don't even think about it." And that's my favorite trait of the Lifestylers I talked to: honesty and straight-forwardness. These people are thinking for themselves and living on their own terms. And boy, do they look like they're having fun!

"People in the Lifestyle come from all walks of life. They're policeman, lawyers, doctors, plumbers, etc. They are ordinary people with extraordinary sex lives." — Rita M., fourth grade teacher

CRITICAL THINKING QUESTION

Is monogamy necessary for a successful marriage?

RECOMMENDED RESOURCE

Swinging from A to Z: A how-to guide from a full-swap Lifestyle couple for enhancing your relationship with recreational sex, by Larry & Mia Fine

POLYAMORY

This is another underground marriage modification movement gaining momentum. Polyamory, meaning "many loves," is the philosophy that it's possible to share romantic love with more than one person at a time. This is not be confused with polygamy, which is marrying multiple people. Where the couples in the Lifestyle are more interested in sex and friendship, the polys, as they are affectionately referred to, are looking for an additional love interest. While sex is certainly a factor, the polys tend to be focused on building significant relationships. Once again, only the emotionally exceptional need apply. As radical as this approach may appear, the premise of their philosophy is worth consideration: why can't someone experience romantic love with more than one person at a time—a sort of "ethical non-monogamy?" Are we so psychologically and emotionally limited that we can't even entertain the idea that our spouse's life may be enhanced by another person? Is our thinking so fear-based that we refuse to overcome our adolescent feelings of possessiveness and jealousy? Are we egotistical enough to believe we have the ability to fulfill every want, need, and desire of our spouse or partner?

"Monogamy sterilizes love and fosters unhealthy codependence, whereas multiple relationships feed off of others' differences and ultimately lead to enriching fulfillment," says Francoise Simpere, author of The Art and Etiquette of Polyamory. "Polyamory accepts the realities of desire without hiding behind the myth of 'one love.' Its model is open-ended and forms itself on the free will and independence of the individual. Its approach is revolutionary and secular: live as you see fit, without imposing your beliefs on others, which runs contrary to the overbearing fundamentalist trend sweeping through societies today." Joan is a 57-year-old poly woman from Atlanta who's been married to Mike for 17 years: "This is my second marriage. My first husband had an affair, and I decided I wasn't going to get married again. Then I met Mike, who introduced me to polyamory. It took me a few months to digest the concept, but it has been one of the most rewarding experiences of my life. I have a wonderful husband and a red hot lover, and they have great respect for one another. Mike is my life partner and Bob is my lover. They are two completely different people and I love them both. Polyamory allows us to live two lives, and everything is open and honest." I interviewed four poly couples and was impressed by their emotional maturity and absence of jealousy. They are nonconformists who have escaped the societal chains that bind us with the guilt, jealousy, and fear of how others might judge us.

The most fascinating aspect of polyamory is how they learn to tame the green monster that lives inside us. After all, polyamory isn't just about sex. This is about being in love with more than one person, so how does the life partner in the triad cope with that? Sam is a 50-year-old heart surgeon from the suburbs of Atlanta who has been polyamorous for nine years. "When my wife and were first exploring polyamory, the idea of her falling in love with another man was beyond my belief system. It screamed self-sabotage. The fact is, it has the opposite effect. The more I let go of my own fears and ego-based need to control and possess her, the more our love grew. It's counterintuitive and nonlinear, but it's the most beautiful, natural phenomenon I've ever experienced. I feel like I'm living a fantasy." I asked him if they ever had fits of jealousy along the way. "Oh, my God! You bet we did! We've both had our moments over the years. Eventually we learned to just let go and love. We gave each other room to make mistakes and grow, and as a result our marriage got stronger and stronger. After nine years of learning, loving, and growing we have a bond that can't be broken. It's amazing."

The coolest thing about the polys is their open-minded approach. It's easy to see this is not an act. The couples I interviewed are thriving because they are growing. "If you believe in personal growth, there's no faster way find it than through the poly life," says Chuck, a 42-year-old lawyer from north Georgia. "It teaches you to operate from a fearless, loved-based consciousness devoid of jealousy."

The delusional thinking about polyamory is that the couples that participate are unhappy in their marriages and searching for someone to replace their partner. The opposite is true. Without a rock solid relationship, there's no way a couple could succeed in this practice. Critical thinking says that only the strongest, most secure couples are capable of even considering this marriage modification. This is clearly an elite class. Like other extreme marriage modifications, polyamory is not for everyone. That being said, the adventure, exhilaration, and emotional fulfillment of romantic involvement with multiple lovers is an exciting and enticing premise. These fearless lovers are ahead of their time and their ideology will continue to attract followers.

There many other marriage modifications, but the four I've described are the most popular. Millions of married couples are making up their own rules and updating an institution that's long overdue for a makeover. The upside of marriage modification, for those who are capable of the skillful navigation necessary, and have the intellectual capacity and emotional maturity to handle it, is success.

The downside is the social penalty these couples will

face if their modifications are made public. When as a nation will we grow up and stop judging people for living their own way? When will the self-righteous finally look in the mirror and ask themselves if they are qualified to make moral judgments about others when they can't even manage their own lives? When will religious leaders wake up and realize they are only human beings who are experts on a book that may have been inspired by God or completely made up? When will they learn that they possess no greater ability to interpret God's will for our lives than anyone else? When will the American public finally embrace the idea that we are all equal and should be free to live our lives as we choose as long as we don't infringe on the rights of others?

Americans are bullied and brainwashed by society to get married, have kids, and live happily ever after. The problem is, so few marriages are happy, and one of the primary reasons is that traditional marriage is an outdated model that refuses to evolve due to societal and religious pressure. So instead of being honest and admitting the marriage model is broken, we pretend everything is fine and cheat, divorce, or remain secretly miserable. It's a sad situation for tens of millions of couples and it's going to get worse until societal and religious dogmas are rejected as the first century philosophy that they are. Men who believed in talking snakes and sea monsters shouldn't be dictating the rules for a 21st century marriage. Unfortunately, Americans are so programmed with religious dogma and superstition from childhood that by the time they enter college they are incapable of thinking for themselves. Christianity is a cult; the biggest and most powerful cult in the world, and it will take years for a powerful enough opposing force to balance the scales. The world will most likely be destroyed by religious extremists before it happens. In the meantime, the marriage modifiers will continue to happily succeed in secret.

★ ★ ★ ★ ★ ★

"Monogamy sterilizes love and fosters unhealthy codependence, whereas multiple relationships feed off of others' differences and ultimately lead to enriching fulfillment." — Francoise Simpere

CRITICAL THINKING QUESTION

Do you believe it's possible to be in love with two people at same time and succeed simultaneously in both relationships?

RECOMMENDED RESOURCE

Polyamory in the 21st Century: Love and Intimacy with Multiple Partners, by Dr. Deborah Anapol

PORNOGRAPHY

Pornography is a multi-billion dollar business in America. In the past 10 years it's gone from taboo to mainstream. Porn stars have become celebrities. The delusions around pornography are many, the biggest being the idea that it's harmful. In a time of unprecedented violence where gangsters are glorified, why would anyone worry about adults watching beautiful people have sex?

Pornography has been around since the beginning of time. The porn craze started with drawings, moved to photographs and eventually, movies. Regardless of the method of delivery, Americans love their porn. Sex is the most popular search word on the Internet, and it's not for health reasons. The most popular and profitable websites on the Internet are porn sites. Once again, it's the moral crusaders who want to ban porn and drive it underground like drugs and prostitution. The critical thinking question is, who are the purveyors and patrons of pornography hurting? Hugh Hefner has been publishing Playboy Magazine since the 1950s and he's still going strong. After 60 years of Playboy, is there any evidence that it's hurt anyone? Can looking at photographs of beautiful women hurt someone? Does porn objectify women? Of course, and so do Hollywood movies, TV commercials, and magazines. Sex sells because we love it. It makes us feel good just thinking about it. It's so deeply embedded in our DNA that we couldn't turn it off if we wanted to. Just ask the one of the hundreds of Catholic priests who molested their congregants. Do you really think these priests set out to hurt kids, defy God, and disgrace themselves? But after years of celibacy, and all of their efforts to harness and hold back the most powerful force in nature, they sought relief in the worst possible way.

Pretending you can create rules and pass laws powerful enough to stop a force like sex is the grandest delusion of all. Bertrand Russell, the brilliant philosopher, said: "Nine-tenths of the appeal of pornography is due to the indecent feelings concerning sex which moralists inculcate in the young; the other tenth is physiological, and will occur in one way or another, whatever the state of the law may be."

Critical thinking says to simply get out of the way and allow people to make their own choices. If they hurt someone else or infringe on their rights, punish them. If not, leave them alone. This is another area where religion and its ego driven leaders are holding America back. If Pat Robertson and his televangelist cronies really want to help people, they should stick to feeding the poor and aiding the sick. That's honorable, and the church has a tremendous track record of charity. But when it comes to telling us how to live, butt out! You are no smarter, well informed or closer to God than the rest of us, so stop insulting us and yourselves by pretending that you are. Pornography will always be popular because it's pleasurable. If you think it's immoral to use it, you have the right to abstain. Others that enjoy it should be free to do so.

"Nine-tenths of the appeal of pornography is due to the indecent feelings concerning sex which moralists inculcate in the young; the other tenth is physiological, and will occur in one way or another, whatever the state of the law may be." — Bertrand Russell

CRITICAL THINKING QUESTION

Should the U.S. Government have the right to tell us what we can watch in the privacy of our own homes?

RECOMMENDED RESOURCE

Prostitution and Pornography: The Philosophical Debate about the Sex Industry, by Jessica Spector

PROSTITUTION

In America, if you pummel your opponent unconscious in a boxing ring, we put your face on a Wheaties box and call you a hero. But if you sell your body for sex, we throw you in jail and call you a whore. In 2012, the oldest profession is still popular and still illegal, though some counties in one state, Nevada, have legal regulated brothels. The delusional thinking is that the government has the right to tell us what we can or cannot do with our own bodies. The critical thinking question is, who owns our bodies, us, or the government? A mixed martial artist can beat someone bloody and even kill them for money, but a woman can't have sex with a man and get paid for it? Is there any level of critical thinking in Washington? NFL football players wrack their bodies for pay. So do hockey players. Why don't we put them in jail? It's because they are sportsmen. This makes no logical sense, but America is a country legislated through emotion. The greatest example is America's addiction to religious dogma. The foundation of our national philosophy is based on a book of symbolic literature written 2,000 years ago by men who believed in talking snakes and sea monsters. This book claims we are the property of God, and therefore he owns our body. So it's OK to sell your body for sport, even if it kills you, but selling it for sex is immoral. This demonstrates a complete lack of critical thought. Think about it: Destroying your mind and body in sport makes you a millionaire, and selling your body for sex makes you a criminal. This is the kind of childish ideology that's destroying America by our refusal to evolve. We lead the world in innovation, but when it comes to social issues we cling to an archaic tome that's been the source of endless wars, destruction, and hatred.

Legalizing prostitution doesn't mean condoning it. No one wants their daughter to be a prostitute. This argument is parallel to saying legalizing drugs would be an endorsement of drugs. No one sane believes drugs are healthy, but that's irrelevant. A lot of things are unhealthy. Should we outlaw cigarettes, junk food, and alcohol, too? We already tried that with alcohol. The 19th amendment banning alcohol is the only Amendment ever to be overturned. Even the President of the United States was drinking alcohol in the White House during prohibition. The bottom line with prostitution is that people love sex, and no law, religion, or imposed morality will stop it. Why does America continue fighting a war it can't win? Why not legalize, regulate, and tax prostitution? The only way to win a fight you can't win is not to fight, and the fact is the government needs the money and could benefit from the savings of court and jail costs.

The moral crusaders determined to save our souls are too rich and powerful to allow us to grow up and evolve. It will happen in time because it's the intelligent choice. Until then, illegal prostitution will continue to grow and the government and religious leaders will continue to pat themselves on the back while some are patronizing prostitutes. I won't waste your time listing the leaders caught in scandals with prostitutes, and we only know about the ones that get caught! The moral hypocrisy in Washington will continue until Americans finally grow up and realize that much of what they see from their so-called leaders is a show. The political and religious power brokers have been controlling the masses in this country for over 200 years, and the manipulation will continue until we begin to think for ourselves. And as long as we continue indoctrinating our children in a philosophy that discourages independent thinking and rewards them for being drones of the church, the abuse will go on. Meanwhile, prostitution will continue, and women will still be subjected to the dangers that accompany it. Prostitutes will be attacked, hurt, and killed because our government doesn't have the guts to legalize it and make it safe. In America, politicians start running for office the day after they're elected, and no one can get elected trying to protect prostitutes.

"Destroying your mind and body in sport makes you a millionaire, and selling your body for sex makes you a criminal. This is the kind of childish ideology that's destroying America by our refusal to evolve."

CRITICAL THINKING QUESTION

Is prostitution illegal in America because it's harmful or because it's perceived as immoral?

RECOMMENDED RESOURCE

Sex For Sale: Prostitution, Pornography, and the Sex Industry, by Ronald Weitzer

ABORTION

I'm happy, yet amazed Roe vs. Wade hasn't been over-turned. It's proof that there are so many people who believe in a woman's right to choose but are only brave enough to admit it when it's law. I don't blame people for being afraid, because taking any social position in America that goes against the religious right can cost you your job, friends, and even family. Religious extremists are a mob you don't want to cross. At least gangs don't pretend to exhibit "Christ-like" behavior. The delusional thinking is that a fetus is a human being. A fetus is only a fetus and it cannot survive without its mother's body, which makes critical thinking on abortion simple: we own our bodies, and neither the government nor the church has any jurisdiction or say in what we do with it. Once it's breathing independently outside the mother's womb it has rights, but until a fetus becomes a human being it is part of its mother's body. The problem with people who argue against this is they are thinking through emotion instead of logic. Abortion is a sad but sometimes neces-sary event, but the mother should be free to choose what happens inside her own body. The fact is that the advent of contraception and legalized abortion has done more to liberate women than any two events in history, and the all-boys club of "women should be kept barefoot and pregnant" is none too pleased. Women have been controlled, bullied, and abused by men since the beginning of time, and maintaining control of their reproductive rights is one of the methods men have used to keep them from rising up in the world. As long as a woman had to be home raising kids, she couldn't go out in the world and stake her own claim or make her own money. Men not only had a physical strength advantage over women, but they enjoyed absolute monetary power as well. It's hard to have equal rights with empty pockets, and unplanned pregnancy was the catalyst of inequality. Birth control and abortion changed all that, and in the past 40 years we have witnessed the greatest emancipation of women in American history. Women now have the power to forge their own destiny, earn unlimited amounts of money, and challenge men for political power. This evolution would never have taken place in America without legalized abortion. Overturning Roe vs. Wade has never been about saving babies. It's about controlling women, and the religious extremists will continue masking this hidden agenda until they are exposed. All a critical thinker has to do is read what the Bible says about women, which treats them as the property of men with about the same status as cattle. Here's what American social activist Elizabeth Cady Stanton said about the treatment of women in the

Bible: "The Bible teaches that women brought sin and death into the world, that she precipitated the fall of the race, that she was arraigned before the judgment seat of Heaven, tried, condemned and sentenced. Marriage for her was to be a condition of bondage, maternity and a period of suffering and anguish, and in silence and subjection, she was to play the role of a dependent on man's bounty for all her material wants, and for all the information she might desire... Here is the Bible position of woman briefly summed up." It baffles me that any woman of even modest education can embrace a book that demeans them to this degree, yet this is the power of delusional thinking. Fortunately, millions of strong independent women refused to be subjected to the tyranny of ancient religious dogma and puritanical societal norms and are boldly creating their own futures. As women continue to gain more political power, social status and financial equality, they will make America a stronger, more prosperous country.

"I don't blame people for being afraid, because taking any social position in America that goes against the religious right can cost you your job, friends, and even family. Religious extremists are a mob you don't want to cross. At least gangs don't pretend to exhibit Christ-like behavior."

CRITICAL THINKING QUESTION

Is the pro-life movement really about protecting life or controlling women in a man's world?

RECOMMENDED RESOURCE

When Abortion was a Crime: Women, Medicine, and Law in the United States 1867-1973, by Leslie J. Reagan

LIVING TOGETHER

Cohabitation and common law marriage have been around for a long time. The delusion is there's something immoral about living with your lover outside of marriage. My wife and I lived together for two years before we married, and it was an exceptional experience. We recently celebrated our 26th wedding anniversary.

When a couple makes the leap from dating to marriage, it's a lousy gamble that rarely pays off. This is one of the reasons divorce, infidelity, and unhappiness are so common. Organized religion bullies people into believing they are going against God by getting to know one another through cohabitation. Life is far more complex than it was 2,000 years ago when pure survival was the primary focus of daily life.

Living together is growing in popularity as the population evolves through higher education and becomes more socially sophisticated. According to research from the University of Denver, about 70% of couples are now cohabiting before marriage. Due to almost unlimited access to knowledge and information, today's teenager knows more about the world than the smartest scholars of 2,000 years ago. Religious leaders' attempts to force society to live by outdated morals through fear mongering is easily recognized by the younger generation. These kids are too well informed to be coerced by fear tactics. This is why we see the new church leaders quickly moving away from sermons of hellfire and damnation, and attempting to draw new followers by softening their message, creating rock bands at church, and using social media to connect with the new generation. Simply put, the more educated a populous becomes, the less effective fear-based messaging is. This is why college professors and other intellectuals are some of the most socially liberal people on the planet. They're too educated to be manipulated by ancient dogma and its puritanical purveyors. Living together is an intelligent trial for marriage before making a lifelong commitment to someone you hardly know. It's hard to admit you married the wrong person after you've had two or three kids, and living together may spare millions of couples a lifetime of emotional agony. Critical thinking says it's only common sense to minimize the risk of making a mistake if you have the choice. Living together accomplishes many things, including heightened emotional intimacy, discovery of one another's personal habits, and maybe most importantly, sexual compatibility. Marrying someone you've never made love to is tempting fate. In fact, sex and intimacy issues are two of the primary causes of divorce. Testing the waters before blindly entering them is common sense. The good news is more couples are living together than ever before; and as more people begin thinking for themselves, this trend will continue to grow.

"My wife and I lived together for two years before we married, and it was an exceptional experience. We recently celebrated our 26th wedding anniversary."

CRITICAL THINKING QUESTION

Is it smart to commit to marrying someone and living with him for the rest of your life without having any evidence that you're still compatible in a closed space?

RECOMMENDED RESOURCE

Unmarried to Each Other: The Essential Guide to Living Together as an Unmarried Couple, by Dorian Solot and Marshall Miller

PREMARITAL SEX

The delusional thinking is that couples should wait until they are married to have sex. Not only is this an unrealistic and ridiculous request, it's a terrible strategy for a successful marriage. Couples who are not sexually compatible are no different than couples who are not otherwise compatible. A sexless marriage is over before it begins. Marriage may be sacred and spiritual, but if a couple isn't hot for one another, it's doomed to fail. To deny the power of sexual attraction to the success of marriage is naïve and foolish. Couples considering marriage should be required to have sex before entering into a lifelong commitment and bringing children into the world. This is common sense in other parts of the world, but in the land of the free, we're reminded that premarital sex is a one-way ticket to hell. If this is true, almost every American is headed south. Unless of course you've repented, which means you can get away with anything as long as you beg forgiveness from God. And we're still falling for this in 2012? Not according to Lawrence Finer, director of domestic research at the Guttmacher Institute, who says, "Premarital sex is normal behavior for the vast majority of Americans, and has been for decades. The data clearly show that the majority of older teens and adults have already had sex before marriage." According to The Economist magazine, 85% of Americans approve of premarital sex. Nevertheless, the fear mongering continues. Critical thinking says we should ignore the voices of archaic doctrine and decide for ourselves.

"Marriage may be sacred and spiritual, but if a couple isn't hot for one another, it's doomed to fail."

CRITICAL THINKING QUESTION

Would you purchase a home without taking a tour; buy a car without a test drive; or choose a church without hearing a sermon?

RECOMMENDED RESOURCE

Premarital Sex in America: How Young Americans Meet, Mate, and Think about Marrying, by Mark Regnerus and Jeremy Uecker

SEX EDUCATION

The delusional thinking is that providing comprehensive sex education in schools is an endorsement of sexual activity. So instead, in the richest country in the world we are forced to learn about sex on the street. Here's objective reality: whether you like it or not, teenagers are going to have sex. They always have and always will. According to America's Center for Disease Control, 46% of high school students are sexually active. And these are only the kids who admit it. The average teenager has been exposed to more sexually explicit movies, games, magazines, and other materials than we have in our entire lives. As much as some Americans would like to hold on, the days of Ozzie and Harriet are over. Teenagers are bombarded by sex, what they are lacking is sex education. They're learning lovemaking through porn. Are we too emotionally immature to educate our kids about one of the most beautiful parts of life? Only 21 states require their public schools to teach sex education, which is an embarrassment for a country that claims to be progressive. Our public school system is still debating whether or not providing condoms in school promotes sexual promiscuity. Condoms don't promote promiscuity, HORMONES promote promiscuity!

Giving students access to condoms doesn't increase their odds of having sex, it just increases the odds that they'll have safe sex. I remember sneaking into a drug store when I was in high school to buy condoms. It was a painful experience because like most Americans, I was programmed in church to be ashamed of my sexual desires. Critical thinking says it's time to pass legislation that mandates comprehensive sex education in all of our public schools.

"Teenagers are bombarded by sex, what they are lacking is sex education. They're learning lovemaking through porn. Are we too emotionally immature to educate our kids about one of the most beautiful parts of life?"

CRITICAL THINKING QUESTION

Can America really claim to have a first-rate school system without comprehensive sex education?

RECOMMENDED RESOURCE

When Sex Goes to School: Warring Views on Sex--and Sex Education-- Since the Sixties, by Kristin Luker

GAY RIGHTS/MARRIAGE

It's time for America to grow up and recognize that homosexuality is neither a choice nor a disease, any more than being a heterosexual is. Homosexuality is a natural predisposition that exists throughout the animal kingdom. Over 50 years ago, Dr. Alfred Kinsey used a sliding scale of 1-6 to prove that all of us have both homo and heterosexual tendencies. Scoring a 6 meant you were primarily homosexual, while a score of 1 meant you were primarily heterosexual. Kinsey believed most people were somewhere in the middle, although many would be afraid to admit it. American society is still suffering from its puritanical roots, and many of our citizens refuse to accept anything that contradicts our cultural norms. The worst offenders are the zealots who claim "God hates fags," and that homosexuals are flawed or immoral human beings. Televangelists like Jerry Falwell and Pat Robertson have poisoned millions with their hate filled tirades against homosexuals. I've watched these bigots mesmerize the masses with laser like precision and wondered, "What would Jesus think? Would the Prince of Peace really endorse this behavior?" How many gay, lesbian and transgender Americans have committed suicide because of their hate filled sermons and broadcasts? How many more are in therapy and gulping anti-depressants because these bullies convinced them they are depraved sinners? In studying mental toughness training for the last 28 years, I've discovered that every one of us has the capacity to be mentally tough. The problem is most of us don't know how to access our toughness, and as a result, people who are operating from a weak state of mind are vulnerable to bullies and bigots. That's why critical thinking demands that the mentally tough stand up for the people who aren't strong enough to stand up for themselves. Would the average American allow a bully to beat up a little kid? No, but that's exactly what we've allowed these religious extremists to do to homosexuals. America has a long history of discrimination that includes blacks, Native Americans, and women. Lincoln freed the slaves and it still took another 100+ years for blacks to be treated like equals. Some people claim racism is still alive and well in modern day America. For all of our country's claims of exceptionalism, we have some pretty shoddy history as it relates to human rights. Sure, we're ahead of most of the world in this area, which is like saying I'm a killer but I killed fewer people than you so I consider my-self exceptional. In a country that claims to be a Christian nation, we have a funny way of demonstrating Christ-like behavior towards minorities. Educated Americans know that homosexuals are no better or worse than anyone

else, and should be left alone to pursue their own version of the American dream. This includes the right to
marry. Religious leaders claim that marriage can only be
between a man and a woman, and that's why they are
against it. This is another far-right fabrication. The real
reason they're against gay marriage is because it would
make gay couples equal to straight couples and remove
the stigma that has been cast upon homosexuality. If the
issue was actually a technicality, could we not make the
case that a two thousand year old mandate be updated?
Furthermore, can the Bible really stand the test of tech-
nical accuracy? It fascinates me how the religious community manipulates the masses with its interpretations
of the Bible. First of all, how does anyone know what the
authors of the Bible we're thinking, much less God himself? Even former President Jimmy Carter, a long time
Sunday School teacher, claimed in an interview with the
Huffington Post that, "God inspired the Bible but didn't
write every word of the Bible." This is a common manipulation tactic designed to empower clergy to embrace the
good parts of the Bible as inspired by God while distanc-
ing themselves from the bad. Carter's church accepts gay
members on an equal basis, but will not allow them to
marry. Is this not akin to allowing blacks to attend school
with whites but insisting they drink from separate water
fountains? I guess we can call it partial bigotry.

Serious thinkers like Thomas Jefferson and Benjamin Franklin understood the idea that the masses need to believe in something beyond this life so badly that they will believe almost anything. Benjamin Franklin was reluctant to discuss his spiritual beliefs in public for this very reason. Toward the end of his life he said he believed in the moral teachings of Jesus but had doubts to his divinity. Jefferson felt the same way and even penned his own version of the Bible called The Jefferson Bible, which is the teachings of Jesus minus any reference to miracles. Here's my point: believe anything you wish to believe. I don't care if you believe in Santa Claus, but the minute you start justifying bigotry, hatred, and violence with your belief you've infringed on the rights of others. The delusional thinking on gay rights and marriage is that it's about protecting the integrity of what's written in the Bible. This is one of the most ridiculous claims ever made, since the Bible is full of evil acts and suggestions we choose to ignore. Where is the integrity in that? Critical thinking says that the church is losing its chokehold on American society and the legalization of gay marriage would deliver another major blow to its eroding power structure. The opposition to gay marriage is all about control and power, and it's just a matter of time before the majority of Americans realize it. Gay marriage will be legal in every state in the country within 10 years because it's the right thing to do. The bullies and bigots will kick and scream like the small minded manipulators they are, but it won't be enough to prevent Americans from doing the right thing. It's time America grew up and welcomed everyone into our culture as an equal and allowed people to their live lives on their own terms.

"Would the average American allow a bully to beat up a little kid? No, but that's exactly what we've allowed these religious extremists to do to homosexuals."

CRITICAL THINKING QUESTION

If religious extremists are so sure God is against homosexuality, why is it so rampant in the animal kingdom he supposedly created?

RECOMMENDED RESOURCE

Gay Marriage: Why it is Good for Gays, Good For Straights and Good for America, By Jonathan Rauch

TRANSGENDER

Some people never get comfortable in their own skin and silently suffer a life of unintentional inauthenticity. They live every day with the guilt and shame our culture stamps on everyone who makes their minority positions public. While many psychologists, psychiatrists, and religious leaders want to use techniques to fix these people, the truth is they were never broken. When people have plastic surgery to improve their appearance, do we stigmatize them and claim they have a psychological disorder? Chaz Bono, formerly Chastity Bono, the daughter-turned-son of singers Sonny and Cher, is a transgender American who is speaking out for all transgenders. "I don't feel it's a mistake that I've had the life I've had," Bono told The Advocate Magazine. "I feel fortunate to be put in front of the camera as a very small child and growing up to be transgender and being able to get this education out there." The delusion is that people like Bono are suffering from a psychological disorder or they have chosen to feel the way they do. The good news is that celebrities like Bono have the platform and ambition to educate Americans. Some religious leaders have spoken out and claimed that being transgender is a sin because it disregards God-given gender distinctions and provides for and promotes homosexuality. They also claim that it dishonors marriage and the home as ordained by God. This is yet another example of how religious leaders in America use their power to control the faithful through guilt and shame. In a study conducted by The National Center for Transgender Equality, 41% of transgenders surveyed had attempted suicide. "These shocking and disheartening numbers speak to the urgency of ending bullying in our nation's schools and discrimination in our workplaces. We know from the recent rash of suicides among young people who have been bullied just how critical it is that we act now and act decisively to save lives," says Rea Carey, executive director of the National Gay and Lesbian Task Force. Whether it's being bullied in school by students and teachers or being labeled a sinner by the church, it's time for Americans to start treating people the way they wish to be treated. Once again I'll pose this Critical Thinking Question:

Would Jesus, or any other serious leader, condone the behavior of bullies and bigots? How many people have to kill themselves before we finally realize we are all equal regardless of color, creed, or sexual orientation? If America is really the beacon of hope that we claim it is, shouldn't that include acceptance and support for people struggling to navigate the trials and tribulations of life? Critical thinking says it's time to reject the religious dogma and societal brainwashing and open our hearts to people of every kind. Isn't life tough enough without our most cherished institutions attacking us for being different? When will the day come when we are all accepted for who we are?

Until that day, America will continue to be a second-rate country when it comes to these important social issues.

*"In a study conducted by The National Center
for Transgender Equality, 41% of transgenders
surveyed had attempted suicide."*

CRITICAL THINKING QUESTION

*Why should those who feel they were born
the wrong gender suffer through life when
they have the opportunity to change?*

RECOMMENDED RESOURCE

*Transgender Explained For Those
Who Are Not,* by Joanne Herman

★   ★   ★   ★   ★   ★   **65**

OBESITY

The delusion of being fat is that it has no impact on a person's sex life. In my 2009 best seller, *Die Fat or Get Tough: 101 Differences in Thinking Between Fat People and Fit People*, I wrote about interviewing 500 fat people and asking them whether or not their spouse was less attracted to them after they gained weight. The majority of people said that being fat had no impact. This is a classic psychological delusion, and millions of Americans are suffering from it. Critical thinking tells us that fat is ugly, unattractive, and unnecessary. We've coddled and babied one another so long in this country when it comes to being fat that we've created a culture of people who refuse to take responsibility for their own failure. The medical community has not helped either. We have doctors telling patients that its genetics, a medical condition, or the government's fault they're fat. These doctors know darn well it's the patients' fault, but they're terrified of losing business and being sued. I've debated doctors on national television over this issue and won every time, because political correctness is no match for objective reality. Not only is fat hazardous to your health, it's the fastest way to destroy your sex life. If you're single, being fat is the best way to insure you'll be sitting home alone on Friday night. I'm not saying this is right or wrong. It is what it is. The world and the people in it don't behave the way we want them to; they behave the way they want to. When you see the world as it is instead of what you wish it was, you move from subjective to objective reality. This gives you the best chance for success. As it relates to obesity, sex, and physical attraction, the best thing you can do to get more of what you want to is to get fit and healthy. You'll look and feel better and you'll have more confidence. You'll feel proud taking your clothes off and getting compliments everywhere you go. The self-esteem among fit people in America is high because they stand out in a country full of fat people who are failing. In physical and sexual terms, fit people are winners, and who doesn't want to be involved with a winner? There is no middle ground on this subject except the degree that you choose to take your level of fitness. Building a body like a professional trainer probably won't make you any sexier than a person with excellent fitness, but denying the sex appeal of the physically fit, or the unattractiveness of the physically unfit, is delusional and self-destructive. Critical thinking embraces the idea that no matter how shallow it seems, our physical appearance is a major attractor or detractor to our lovers. We have little power over our looks, but when it comes to our body weight, we have 100% control. The bottom line is the fastest way to improve your love life is to get fit.

"Not only is fat hazardous to your health, it's the fastest way to destroy your sex life. If you're single, being fat is the best way to insure you'll be sitting home alone on Friday night."

CRITICAL THINKING QUESTION

Is a red-hot sex life worth dropping your extra weight?

RECOMMENDED RESOURCE

Die Fat or Get Tough: 101 Differences in Thinking Between Fat People and Fit People, by Steve Siebold

CHILDLESS (BY CHOICE) COUPLES

The delusion is that couples who choose to remain childless are self-centered, shallow, and self-absorbed. The fact is more couples are choosing to be childfree. Societal programming and pressure are becoming less prominent as a new generation of adults begins to question their parents' beliefs and values. In 1990, 4.3% of American women said they were voluntarily childless. By 2002, that number had climbed to 6.2%. Many experts believe this trend will continue as women earn more money and have more choices. "What a lot of people forget is that childlessness was not an option for so much of human history," says author and historian Elaine Tyler May. "Your choice was celibacy or children." Birth control has been available in one form or another for 130 years, but has been blocked by both government and religious groups. It took the U.S. Government until 1965 to shoot down the last state law (Connecticut) prohibiting the use of contraceptives. The Roman Catholic Church has provided the main religious group opposition. Luckily, society is evolving, and people are getting more educated and are starting to think for themselves. Women are no longer subservient to men and they are taking control of their own destinies. Remaining childfree is becoming a more attractive option for more women. Laura S. Scott, author of *Two is Enough: A Couples Guide to Living Childless by Choice*, sums it up beautifully: "So why is it that when we think of families, we still think of Mom and Dad and the 2.5 kids? Because it remains our cultural ideal, and we cling to it like a baby to a blanket." Critical thinking dictates that the decision to have a child or live child-free should be made consciously, minus societal, family, or religious pressure or guilt. Some people live to raise kids. It's their life's dream, and these are the people who should have kids. We need more parents who actually want to raise a happy, healthy family. For others, like me, we have no interest in it. My wife and I have been married and childfree (by choice) for 26 years, and we are two of the happiest people on earth. We're free to live on a beautiful northern lake in the spring and summer, while escaping to South Florida for the winter. Our business requires that we travel the world, and we spend the time in between speeches and media appearances enjoying the sights. Being childfree and financially independent allows us to live what author/philosopher Ayn Rand called, "An unrestricted existence." This is not a lifestyle for every-one, but I don't know anyone who wouldn't like to try it. That being said, people with kids will often push back on couples like us and say; "You're missing out on the greatest gift of life—children." And maybe they're right. It would be delusional to say that the childfree couple isn't missing out on a unique experience. Of course we are. It's simply a matter of opportunity cost, because the couples with kids are missing out on living an unrestricted existence, or at least a version of it. That's objective reality. Which lifestyle is better? I don't know. But critical thinking says that while having kids has always been the norm, childless couples are not the selfish, self-absorbed people they are sometimes portrayed to be.

"In 1990, 4.3% of American women said they were voluntarily childless. By 2002, that number had climbed to 6.2%. Many experts believe this trend will continue as women earn more money and have more choices."

CRITICAL THINKING QUESTION

Have you made a conscious or unconscious decision to have children or remain childfree?

RECOMMENDED RESOURCE

Two is Enough: A Couples Guide to Living Childless, by Choice by Laura S. Scott

SEX ADDICTION

The delusion is that people with a high sex drive are suffering from an addiction. The subject of sex in America is approached through emotional instead of logical thinking, which often leads to irrational conclusions. Sex addiction is an example. Unemotional critical thinking tells us that sex is the most powerful force in nature. Without the primal urge to procreate, the world as we know it would not exist. Are there people with emotional problems who use sex like a drug to medicate themselves? Of course. And these people need help. But to label them sex addicts is like calling an avid golfer a golf addict. Or a woman who owns 200 pairs of shoes a shoe addict. The word addiction is so overused in American society that it no longer carries credibility. Hollywood stars like David Duchovny, and professional athletes like Tiger Woods, get caught cheating on their spouses and are automatically labeled sex addicts. Critical thinking says that money, celebrity, and power give men access to unlimited sex from unlimited people, and right or wrong, some of them take advantage of it. The moral outrage expressed by the masses leads us to another example of delusion, which is the idea that many people who criticize the cheaters would also cheat given the chance. There's an old saying that's been passed down among men through the ages, and while it's crude, it's also true for the majority of the male populous. The saying is: that men consciously or subconsciously place all women in two categories;the ones they would have sex with and the ones that they wouldn't. Most men would never admit this publicly, yet it's a common topic of conversation when men gather in social circles. It's so crude that it's funny, and so true that it's scary, and it probably applies equally to women. The fairer sex would probably articulate it more eloquently, but it's all the same. The exception to this line of thinking are the men with deep religious or spiritual roots whose beliefs forbid or prevent them from the objectification of another human being. This is a positive example of how dedication to a higher power often (but not always) elevates the faithful above lust and related base desires. The question is do we really have to believe in a supernatural being to elevate our level of thinking? Some of the most disciplined priests, parishioners, and servants have fallen prey to the animal desire that smolders below the surface. This goes all the way to the White House, and it dates back centuries before Bill Clinton and Monicagate. Some of our most beloved national leaders would be labeled sex addicts if they were alive today. Sex therapists would have had a field day with American icons such as Thomas Jefferson, Benjamin Franklin, Alexander

Hamilton, Franklin D. Roosevelt, and John F. Kennedy. Critical thinking can't deny the influence that sex has had on many of our most influential and respected leaders. You could even make the argument that without an extraordinary sex drive, these men would not have made history. Powerful, ambitious people are often highly sexed, but this doesn't make them addicts. According to Helen Fisher, the biological anthropologist and a member of the Center for Human Evolutionary Studies in the anthropology department at Rutgers, "Along with ambition comes a high sex drive. Testosterone's linked with both of them." The sexual addiction label is yet another example of how American society attempts to complicate the simple.

"Some of our most beloved national leaders would be labeled sex addicts if they were alive today. Sex therapists would have had a field day with American icons such as Thomas Jefferson, Benjamin Franklin, Alexander Hamilton, Franklin D. Roosevelt, and John F. Kennedy."

CRITICAL THINKING QUESTION

If so many of America's most influential leaders were not hyper-sexed, would the United States be the economic powerhouse it is; and furthermore, would a free America even exist?

RECOMMENDED RESOURCE

One Nation Under Sex: How the Private Lives of Presidents, First Ladies and Their Lovers Changed the Course of American History, by Larry Flynt and David Eisenbach

TANTRA

The word tantra comes from ancient Sanskrit language meaning "expansion through awareness." Tantra is a spiritual process designed to quiet the mind and activate sexual energy. Tantra originated in India, Nepal, and China. It's an amazing experience that elevates a person's consciousness far beyond the physical act of making love. The tantric process involves breathing, sounds, and movements that create an altered state of sexual and non-sexual consciousness. While pornography often promotes sexuality through the objectification of the female and male forms, tantra promotes respect and even worship of both the male and female spirit that transcends the body. It celebrates the sexual union as an honoring of all beings and creation. After interviewing 26 couples who attended a Tantra workshop lead by world-renowned master Charles Muir, I was awestruck at the positive effect this practice had on people. One couple, who asked to remain anonymous, said "It's taken our entire relationship to a whole new level. It's not just about sex. It's about the way you think about and care for your partner." Another couple from Chicago had similar thoughts: "We were married for 24 years before we discovered this ancient practice.

Tantra has literally changed our lives." Not one couple I interviewed had a negative thing to say. I was so impressed I decided to attend a beginners' workshop in Boston with my wife, and we were both amazed. The people criticizing this process couldn't have possibly studied it. It's one of the most spiritual, consciousness-elevating processes I've ever experienced. The biggest role sex plays is the use of its energy to heighten your awareness and bring you into a more joyous state of mind. The whole process is people and life-affirming, and there is no downside. So where is the delusional thinking in this all positive practice? Once again, the delusion and misrepresentation comes from the world of religious fundamentalism. These zealots have always been fearful of anything that expands the thinking of their congregation beyond their weekly sermon. The more educated and sophisticated their congregants become, the less control they have over their minds—and wallets. Here's what one religious blog had to say:

"If Christians begin to incorporate their contemplative proclivities with their sexual lives (a Christian version of tantric sex), the results will be devastating to the church, and we predict sexual perversion will be more rampant than ever. Why? Because if the altered states of consciousness are truly demonic realms (as we believe they are) then tantric sex is another venue of the hidden darkness that Jesus spoke of."

This is a prime example of how paranoid some of these leaders are. They fear anything that empowers people and gives them conscious control of their lives. Any practice that is a catalyst for altered states of consciousness is a threat, including meditation, reiki, floating, yoga, and dozens of others. The good news is some of the new religious leaders are actively promoting self-awareness, such as ministers like Rick Warren of the Saddleback Church in Southern California. The New Thought Churches, such as Unity and Science of Mind Centers, lead the way with their focus on positive thinking, prosperity, and the expansion of human consciousness. The New Thought Churches arguably have the most progressive religious leaders, and hopefully more will evolve into the 21st century and embrace human empowerment. Church participation has been declining for years in America, and the primary reason is the increasing access to information and education. The younger generation of Americans refuse to be bullied by the church. They're simply too smart and they see the mass manipulation of the religious community on their parents' generation and refuse to fall victim to it. This is sad for society, because the church at its best is one of the greatest contributors to society. If it adapts to the times and takes its focus off the supernatural, it will once again begin to thrive and grow. If not, it will continue to decline into an archaic relic of the past. Critical thinking says that in a time of unprecedented change, the only institutions that will survive will be the ones that can embrace change. Tantra is a force for good, as it celebrates the human spirit and honors the union of lovers. Critical thinking says try it and decide for yourself.

"Tantra is a force for good, as it celebrates the human spirit and honors the union of lovers."

CRITICAL THINKING QUESTION

Why is the expansion of the human spirit so threatening to religious extremists?

RECOMMENDED RESOURCE

Tantric Love: A Nine Step Guide to Transforming Lovers into Soul Mates, Ma Ananda Sarita and Swami Anand Geho

CONTRACEPTION

Contraception has probably done more to liberate and empower American women than any other single event. Brilliant women like Margaret Sanger, founder of Planned Parenthood, devoted her life to fighting for the right for access to safe and legal contraception. Today, 99% of American women use contraception at some point in their lives. But it wasn't always this way. In the late 1800s, women were giving birth to 8 to 10 children, with no way to prevent pregnancy outside of abstinence. Margaret Sanger, a nurse who had witnessed too many unwanted pregnancies, opened the first birth control clinic in 1916, designed to educate and empower women so they could take control of their own bodies and futures. It was closed down shortly after opening, but the gutsy Sanger fought back and the first legal birth control clinic opened in 1923. Contraception has taken many forms since, but the breakthrough that changed the world was the 1960 creation of the birth control pill. Margaret Sanger, who died in 1966, lived just long enough to see the pill legalized in 1965. This gave women an unprecedented level of control over their lives. They were now empowered to plan their lives without the burden or risk of pregnancy.

They were free to launch careers outside the home and even to choose whether or not to have children at all. Men had ruled America since its founding, and the pill was the beginning of the rise and equalization of women. The bottom line is that the pill gave women choices they never had before, and you can probably guess who wasn't very happy about it. That's right, the Church. Religious leaders denounced the pill saying it would destroy morality and promote promiscuity, and that delusional thinking continues to this day. Nearly 50 years after the pill was legalized, women are no less moral but far more powerful. Unemotional critical thinking could have predicted this back in 1965, but this has not been the Church's greatest strength throughout history. Their goal is control through manipulation, guilt, and fear, and contraception is another battlefield in which they have lost. The most vehement opponent of contraception has been the Catholic Church, whose only answer to birth control is abstinence. These religious leaders honestly believe they can guilt and shame women in the 21st century from having sex, and it's one of the reasons their numbers are declining. In February, 2012, The Washington Post reported that 98% of sexually active Catholic women age 15 to 44 use birth control, and the church might as well realize they are not going to stop the most powerful force on earth. Thanks to inventions like the Internet, Americans are far too informed to fall for threats of hellfire and damnation. The world has evolved, and if the Church and its leadership is being left behind, it's their own fault.

The pill now generates 3.5 billion dollars in sales per year, and is more popular than ever. There are 40 different brands of the pill and more in development, including various forms of male birth control medications. Like the delusions of the drug war, which states that legalizing drugs will set off an epidemic of drug addicted people, religious leaders were certain that the legalization of contraception would create a society of rampant promiscuity. Fifty years later, the results are in: it didn't. As a matter fact, there is no evidence that the pill changed sexual behavior in any way, outside of family planning. The critics were wrong again, yet they still insist that passing out condoms or any form of birth control promotes promiscuity. Apparently, science and evidence are not valued by church leaders. They believe it's better to have people die of AIDS than pass out condoms. Dr. Andrea Tone, a contraception historian and scholar on women's health said this: "50 years ago sex was extremely taboo, culturally. It was so taboo that TV shows were not allowed to depict the master bedroom of the house with anything but double beds in a sterile setting." Then came the pill, followed by the sexual revolution and open rebellion to control and manipulation. It wasn't a perfect progression, but it was progress. Today, we have women running Fortune 500 companies, becoming self-made millionaires, and raising beautiful healthy families...all by choice, with or without the consent of men. In the near future, America will elect a female president, and for the first time in history a woman will be the most powerful person in the world. Don't expect the old church establishment or the good old boys club to embrace it or help make it happen. On the contrary, they will kick and scream with all their might. But in the end, they will lose. This will catapult all women to heights of credibility and respect the likes of which they've never seen. We've already seen how the election of Barack Obama lifted the African-American community, and even though I didn't vote for Obama because I don't like his politics, I was overjoyed at how blacks around the world rejoiced at the ascension of one of their own. Whether or not you agree with his politics, the election of our first black president was a day to be celebrated. It will be the same when we elect our first female president, and without the pill, it probably wouldn't have happened.

"In February, 2012 The Washington Post reported that 98% of sexually active Catholic women age 15 to 44 use birth control."

CRITICAL THINKING QUESTION

With the overwhelming popularity of birth control, why does the Catholic Church refuse to fully embrace it?

RECOMMENDED RESOURCE

Catholics and Contraception: An American History, by Leslie Woodcock Tentler

PLANNED PARENTHOOD

Planned Parenthood is the largest provider of reproductive healthcare in the United States which includes, among many services, contraception, comprehensive sex education, and abortions. The organization boasts over 800 clinics in the United States with an annual budget of one billion dollars. Planned Parenthood has received federal funding since 1970, when Richard Nixon signed the Family Planning Services and Population Research Act into law. They receive around 350 million dollars a year in federal funds. Planned Parenthood has more than four million activists, supporters, and donors nationwide. They are the largest provider of sex education in America and they have performed over four million breast exams in the past five years. Contraception accounts for 35% of their total services, while abortions account for 10%. Planned Parenthood empowers women to take control of their own reproductive health and gives them the choice to control their own bodies. They endure endless attacks and criticism from fundamentalists and right-wing conservatives who attempt to discredit them any way they can, up to and including outright lies. Senator Orrin Hatch stated that 95% of what Planned Parenthood does is abortions. He was only 92% off the actual statistic. Radical radio host Alex Jones called Planned Parenthood a "Nazi organization." And those are just a few examples of the lengths that social conservatives will go to destroy Planned Parenthood's reputation. The delusional thinking is that this conspiracy is about Planned Parenthood. It's not. Critical thinking says it's about ultimately overturning Roe vs. Wade and legalized abortion. It's about control over women. These control freaks masked as moral crusaders want to tell women what they can and can't do with their own bodies. The conservatives in government and the religious leaders from the far right think they know what's best for women, but since women aren't listening, they want to outlaw their right to ignore them. Then if women don't listen they'll simply throw them in jail. The sickest part of the story is how they mask their ambition by claiming that banning abortion is about saving babies. These people will say and do anything to force us to comply to their version of morality. The destruction of Planned Parenthood and legalized abortion wouldn't stop abortions any more than the drug war has stopped drug use. Women will have abortions, and if they are illegal they will have them in back rooms and dark places. The poor will revert back to using coat hangers. Supreme Court Justice Ruth Bader Ginsburg said this in response to making abortion illegal: "We've been there before and we're not going back." She's correct. We have been there before and it didn't work, which is why we changed it. Maybe the religious extremists would like to reinstate prohibition as well? And while we're at it, why don't we repeal a woman's right to vote? Don't laugh, because the religious zealots are capable of any of these things. They would just as soon women were seen and not heard. And they would appreciate if you followed what it says in the Bible about being submissive to your husband. These are conversations we're still having in America, and that's what's killing us. We must evolve or be replaced by a country that will. If Planned Parenthood and legal abortion are eliminated, it could cause a domino effect that could set this country back 50 years. I applaud Planned Parenthood for empowering women and support them in their fight to survive the attacks of the socially backward.

"Planned Parenthood has more than four million activists, supporters and donors nationwide. They are the largest provider of sex education in America."

CRITICAL THINKING QUESTION

If it's not about overturning Roe v. Wade and controlling women, why would religious extremists be so passionate about eliminating an organization that helps millions of young couples control their lives and plan their futures?

RECOMMENDED RESOURCE

Sacred Work: Planned Parenthood and Its Clergy Alliances, By Tom Davis

DIVORCE AND REMARRIAGE

Divorce and remarriage is as common in America as baseball and apple pie. When you consider the marriage premise, it's pretty easy to see why. The idea that one person can fulfill all of your emotional, physical, intellectual, spiritual, and sexual needs is patently naïve. Americans are not used to settling for second best, and as a result, they often jump ship and try their luck with someone else. Add kids into the equation and you have a mess. The fact is marriage is a failure as an institution and it's getting worse. In his book, *Marriages, Families & Intimate Relationships*, Brian K. Williams writes that married adults now divorce two-and-a-half times as often as they did 20 years ago and four times as often as they did 50 years ago. Between 40% and 60% of new marriages will end in divorce. A serious percentage of the couples who stay married are cheating. Estimates vary, but some experts say the number could be as high as 40%. Another percentage of couples are forced to stay together due to money problems, and others stick it out for kids. What's left is the small percentage of happily married couples. The delusional thinking around divorce and remarriage is that there's something wrong with it, and that one or both parties is at fault. Even in 2012 America, there's still a stigma attached to divorce. It's viewed as a failure to some and a sin to others. But the complexity of marriage, especially with children, can be extreme, and the best solution may be divorce. The delusion is exacerbated by religious dogma that commands couples to stay together no matter how unhappy they are, unless they have evidence of fornication or "abandonment from an unbeliever." The guilt the church has inflicted on couples is criminal. Many people have enough trouble with self-esteem issues without being scolded on Sunday for being a sinner. Pastor John Piper says this: "The Bible does not allow for divorce or remarriage...ever." And he's not alone. Many clergy members preach the same intolerance. Critical thinking says that if something isn't working and you can't fix it, end it. Religious leaders love to talk about the afterlife and how great it's going to be, but until they have evidence to prove it, all we have is this life. Why waste it in a marriage that isn't working? When I interviewed God-Centered Marriage advocate Jay Travis, he insisted that the problem with modern society is that we treat marriage like dating. And maybe he's right in the sense that it's easier than ever to get divorced. I'm all for working on your marriage and trying to make it work. But if you're miserable, and divorce is the best solution, critical thinking says get divorced guilt free and move on with your life. After all, none of us knows how long we have, and there is certainly no evidence that we're going to get a second chance. The same thing applies to remarrying. If you decide to marry again and you find the right person, consider yourself lucky. The problem with divorce, remarriage, and many of the social issues we face in America today, is the cloud of delusion that organized religion casts on them, causing confusion, guilt, and depression. Any serious level of conformity to religious doctrine requires the willing full suspension of critical thinking. The advice we deliver at Mental Toughness University is "think for yourself." You're responsible for your own happiness, and if divorce is the best answer, get divorced and don't look back.

"Married adults now divorce two-and-a-half times as often as they did 20 years ago and four times as often as they did 50 years ago. Between 40% and 60% of new marriages will end in divorce."

CRITICAL THINKING QUESTION

How can marriage be the foundation of American society with a 50% divorce rate and a substantial percentage of couples who are unhappily married?

RECOMMENDED RESOURCE

World-Class Marriage and Infidelity Coach Suzie Johnson can be reached at www.goasksuzie.com.

INTERRACIAL MARRIAGE

As America has become more of a melting pot, inter-racial marriage has flourished. Before 1970, only 2% of marriages were interracial. Now the number is closer to 15%, and experts say this number will continue to grow. The breakthrough began back in 1958, when Richard and Mildred Loving, an interracial couple who were mar-ried and living in Virginia, were arrested and jailed for the crime of marrying someone of another race. And that's not the most unbelievable part of the story. The judge in the case upheld the arrest and stated: "God put different races on different continents for a reason." That gives you an idea of where America stood on racial issues in 1958. The good news is that the Lovings refused to quit and took their case all the way to the Supreme Court which overturned the decision in 1967. It took nine years, but Loving vs. Virginia became a landmark case that made history. It paved the way for millions of interracial couples thriving today. The truth is Americans have become more tolerant of diversity, but the delusional thinking is that discrimination against interracial marriage doesn't exist. It exists, and the numbers are staggering. According to a CBS News poll, 40% of Americans are against interracial marriage. That's 130 million people. Scary, isn't it? In a March 14, 2012, survey of Republican voters in Alabama, 21% said interracial marriage should be illegal. Granted, Alabama probably isn't known for progressive thinking, but it's frightening to think that many voters, who tend to be more educated than non-voters, still see something wrong in the coupling of races in 2012. In December, 2011, The Gulnare Baptist Church in Kentucky banned mixed race couples from being members. Critical thinking says that while we've made great strides in race relations, the stigma still exists, and there is more work to be done. As America continues to become more diverse, we need to continue beating the drum of racial equality and desegregation through education in schools, public service platforms and especially in churches. The more we do, the stronger our country will become.

"According to a CBS News poll, 40% of Americans

are against interracial marriage."

CRITICAL THINKING QUESTION

Why are millions of Americans afraid and
intolerant of people of different races?

RECOMMENDED RESOURCE

Love's Revolution: Interracial
Marriage, by Maria Root

POLITICS

POLITICS IN AMERICA

Our leaders in Washington are lost. Democrats are creating a nanny state while Republicans are promoting puritanical dogma. The net result is America is losing ground. In order to maintain our superpower status, we need to elect mentally tough politicians capable of critical thinking.

From the financial disaster of Obama Care to the social bigotry towards the gay rights movement, we have elected leaders who are either fiscally or socially irresponsible. It's time to send serious leaders to Washington to solve the complex problems we face in the 21st century while simultaneously moving forward toward creating a more socially progressive, self-reliant society.

The fundamental question we must answer is who should be running our lives and dictating how we live. The democrats believe government should make the rules and the republicans believe in self-reliance overseen by a supernatural dictator. I'm generalizing, of course, but these are the two most powerful political philosophies in Washington, neither of which is good for America or

American's.

The political philosophy that will catapult America back to the top is one of smaller government; a true separation of church and state and a doctrine of non-interference in the personal affairs of our citizens. In short, the government should protect us from foreign enemies, provide a reasonable safety net for the less fortunate and enforce laws that punish people for hurting others. In essence, government should refrain from providing services people can provide for themselves or can be delivered by the private sector. America is a country that was founded on independence and free thinking, yet somehow we've lost our way. It's time for Americans to rise up and challenge our political leaders and take control of the direction of our beloved nation. We're running out of time, and the longer we wait the less chance we have of succeeding. I believe we can do it, and I'll bet you do, too. Let's hope we're right, because the fate of the world rests in our hands.

UNIONS

Unions are another archaic American institution that served a purpose in a bygone era and should to be buried with the dead. Don't get me wrong, there was a time when employers abused their power, and unions leveled the playing field through leverage. They gave the little guy a voice, and it worked. Fortunately, the days of businesses running rough-shod over workers are gone. In the era of Twitter, Facebook, cell phones with cameras, and 24 hour news, the power is in the hands of the people. Joe lunch bucket, who 20 years ago needed a union to be heard, now has the power to cause a national uproar if he is mistreated in any way. This is a good thing, yet we have a new problem—the union leaders and members who refuse to give up their stranglehold on industry and government. Union workers have become spoiled with inflated wages, tenure, and guaranteed work based on every factor outside of job performance and results. The abuse of power is now coming from the unions instead of employers. I grew up around unions in Chicago in the 1960s and '70s, and most of my family members were in a union. In terms of technological advancement, that's 100 years ago. We are living in a very different work environment than the 1970s.

Today, our business operates in almost every state in the country, and we do everything possible to avoid doing business in unionized states. 15 years ago I was working in Cleveland with a crew of non-union workers on a three month, two million dollar project that was running smoothly. One day after the crew left the plant, I was approached by a business agent from a local union who threatened to sabotage our project unless I fired my crew and hired workers from his local union hall. I refused, and luckily he was bluffing, but it didn't keep him from coming around our job site so often that I called the police. The same thing happened to us in Seattle. It was like something you see in movies from the 1930s, when intimidation ruled and people got hurt. The thing that shocked me most was that these people truly believed their union workers were entitled to jobs on our project simply because they lived in that town. The business agents told me I had an obligation to hire his members, and I would regret it if I didn't. This is the same mob rules mentality union workers who cross picket lines face when they decide feeding their family is more important than the demands of the union. They're threatened, slandered, and ostracized for going to work. And this is still going on in 2012! The unions that were created to protect the little guy from the bully have become the bully. Beyond this third grade mentality of bullying is the entitlement to jobs unions promote and their members actually believe. The private sector has weeded out most of this nonsense in recent years, with unions only representing 7.5% of private sector employees. But the public sector is still bloated with 43% of public employees represented by unions. I was being interviewed on television about my last book a few months ago in Madison, Wisconsin, when Governor Scott Walker was challenging the teachers' union. Walker displayed world-class mental toughness in the face of having his life and livelihood threatened by the same people who educate Wisconsin's children. You'd think professional educators would be above such scare tactics, and while many of them probably are, it doesn't take many death threats to make it a serious situation. Governor Walker eliminated collective bargaining rights, which is how unions blackmail employers into doing what they want. Again, in the past this was probably necessary. Not anymore. I happened to be doing a live television interview on CBS in Madison, Wisconsin, outside of the capitol building during the teachers' protests, and I talked to more than a dozen teachers. All of them told me the same thing: they said they had the right to collective bargaining and to their job. When I asked them where job performance fit into the equation, I barely got a reply. They looked at me as though they didn't understand the question. And that's one of the biggest problems unions create: the idea that they have a right to a job, like it's an entitlement awarded at birth. And these are smart people, professional educators, many with advanced degrees. These are the people spending eight hours a day with our kids and they honestly believe the government owes them a job. Dr. Caroline Hoxby, from Stanford University, says: "Teachers matter a lot. In fact, research shows that teachers matter more than anything else in a school. We need flexibility to find and retain good teachers. The typical collective bargaining contract in the U.S. says you must pay every teacher the same amount if she has the same credentials and experience. Collective bargaining contracts are opposed to merit pay and methods of getting unsuccessful teachers out of the classroom." James Sherk, a labor policy analyst, said this in an interview with The Heritage Foundation: "Collective bargaining raises the costs of providing services. Congress shouldn't be making those decisions for the state." This is why I applaud Governor Walker for persisting and doing the right thing for Wisconsin. He set an example for Governors nationwide. It's inspiring to see that we still have leaders who are willing to stand up for what's good for America.

The future belongs to the states who become right-to-work states where unions have no power and cannot bully businesses into hiring workers simply because they live in the neighborhood and pay dues. As a private employer,

I've hired hundreds of people over the years, and the only state I'd open a new business or move my existing business to is a right-to-work state. As of this writing, Governor Mitch Daniels of Indiana has just signed legislation to make Indiana the 23rd right-to-work state in the country. Minnesota Congressman Steve Drazkowski and Senator Dave Thompson are currently working on creating a constitutional amendment to do the same for the state of Minnesota. As an employer doing business in Minnesota, this motivates me to hire more workers there, and that's the intended result: job creation. The delusional thinking on unions is that they are necessary in modern-day America. Critical thinking says they served their purpose in the past, and it's time for them to go. If you want to earn more money, bullying your employer with a mob isn't the answer. Production is. If you want to earn more money, provide more service. End of story. That's critical thinking.

"If you want to earn more money, bullying your employer with a mob isn't the answer. Production is. If you want to earn more money, provide more service. End of story. That's critical thinking."

CRITICAL THINKING QUESTION

When will America evolve from the union's chokehold and its mob rules mentality?

RECOMMENDED RESOURCE

Government Unions and the Bankrupting of America, by Daniel DiSalvo

SOCIAL SECURITY

President Franklin D. Roosevelt created the Social Security act in 1935. The level of poverty this era witnessed during the Great Depression was terrifying. People living in tents and shanties, starving in the streets, and jumping out of buildings. Many of us with depression-era parents were raised on the stories of financial hardship and misery that younger generations only read about in history books. As a pro-capitalist and free enterprise advocate, I should be lashing out against this taxpayer-funded, unbelievably expensive, social welfare program. But in the interest of intellectual honesty, I simply cannot. As much as I believe in self-responsibility, the fact is that without Social Security we would have millions of senior citizens living on the streets. Is it our responsibility as a society to pay the bills of the old and poor? No. Are we really obligated to be our brother's keeper? I don't think so. That being said, in the specific instance of Social Security, it seems like the right thing to do. My libertarian-leaning friends don't appreciate my position, and I understand their point. America is not a socialist country, and Social Security is socialism. I get that. In a truly free country that operates with a free market, we are individually responsible to save our money and take care of ourselves without being a burden to the state or anyone else. Any freedom-loving American will agree with the concept that in a perfect world, this is ideal. The problem is we don't live in a perfect world. People get sick. They lose money. And sometimes it's their fault and other times it's not. The economic collapse of 2008 is an example. The foundation of the problem was banks approving mortgages for people who couldn't afford them. Some make the argument that the borrowers are responsible for knowing what they can afford. I agree. Banks are in the business of making loans the way stores are in the business of selling goods. The problem the public wasn't responsible for was the collapse of the housing market and subsequent economic fallout. Millions of American families that had a substantial portion of their net worth in the equity of their homes saw their wealth disappear overnight. Others lost their homes to foreclosure and even more are underwater. Adding to the problem is high unemployment. My point is that some of these problems are self-inflicted and others are not. As a means of bridging the gap, a revamped and fiscally sound Social Security system can serve as a safety net for people who fall between the cracks. The rest of us don't need it and shouldn't collect it. I realize this is a socialistic strategy. So be it. We're not talking philosophy; we're talking about life and death. And it's not a zero-sum equation. Many of us are one bad break from bankruptcy, and others have more money than they can spend. This is not about penalizing the rich. Not even close. I applaud the millionaires and billionaires who have boldly staked their claim and made their American dream come true. They are heroes to be celebrated. All I'm saying is that while it's easy to claim that we are all competing for financial prosperity on a level playing field, it simply isn't true. Not everyone is born with the brain of a Bill Gates, the investing intellect of a Warren Buffet, or the business savvy of a Donald Trump. Most of us possess average intellect, education, and talent, and we go to work every day and do the best we can. Few of us become millionaires. Are some people just lazy and undisciplined? Sure, but only a small percentage. Most of us work hard to be successful and self-reliant. But what about the guy who works hard and just gets a bad break? What about the gal who's on her way to great things and gets sick? Just for a second, let's forget ideology and consider decency. Even though we don't owe these people, isn't it the right thing to do? If we have a chance to reduce the suffering of another human being, shouldn't we take it? The delusional thinking is that it can't be funded without large tax increases. It can, and if we elect a critical thinker to the Presidency who can convince Congress, it will. Critical thinking says the age when people start collecting must be raised to match our ever increasing lifespan. In addition, a national campaign should be launched to inspire wealthy Americans to donate their Social Security check back to the system to serve the people who need it. Not only should these wealthy Americans be rewarded with a 100% tax deduction, they should be publically recognized for their success and patriotism. Napoleon said it best, "Men will die for ribbons." Donating your Social Security check back to the system should be seen as a badge of honor, status symbol, and even a positive trapping of success. If at any time the person needed to collect from the system, they could re-enroll without any questions. They wouldn't get back any funds that they donated, but they would get their monthly check moving forward. This would become a source of pride for many people, and they would inspire one another to join the club. We need to stop debating whether or not we can afford this necessary program and engage in critical thinking to fix it. If America is truly an exceptional country, we are obligated to protect the weakest among us. Once we stop the bipartisan bickering and begin thinking at a higher level, we will make it happen.

"Is it our responsibility as a society to pay the bills of the old and poor? No. Are we really obligated to be our brother's keeper? I don't think so. That being said, in the specific instance of Social Security, it seems like the right thing to do."

CRITICAL THINKING QUESTION

How can the richest country in the world be unable to find a way to fund our most sweeping social safety net?

RECOMMENDED RESOURCE

Social Security: The Inside Story, 2012 Edition, by Andy Landis

STEM CELL RESEARCH

Stem cell research offers some of the most exciting potential scientific breakthroughs in history. No one has an
issue with somatic (adult) stem cell research, but when
it comes to embryonic stem cells, religious leaders have
attempted to block this life-changing research every step
of the way. Embryonic stem cells are harvested from
human embryos, and their amazing potential lies in the
fact that they can become any kind of cell which ultimately has the power to cure diseases like Alzheimer's,
Lou Gehrig's, Parkinson's, spinal cord injuries, and others. Adult stem cell research has been going on for 50
years, while embryonic stem cell research is only about
12 years old. Much of this time has been wasted due to
the constant intervention from the religious right, the
biggest hero being former President George W. Bush, who
banned federal funding of embryonic stem cell research
during his presidency. This is yet another example of how
organized religion blocks human progress and leaves the
sick and struggling to continue suffering when potential
cures could be right around the corner. Instead of em-
bracing scientific study and funding it, they suggest the
sick simply pray to God for the cure. A God for which

no scientific evidence exists. Luckily, President Barack Obama overturned Bush's foolishness and reinstated federal funding for this crucial work. The delusional thinking in this equation is simple: Religious extremists say that only God has the right to terminate a human life. Once again, they are speaking for a God for which no proof exists. They would rather protect a dead embryo than offer a cure to millions of suffering human beings who are alive and breathing. Make no mistake: this is not about attacking organized religion. As Americans, you and I are free to believe anything we want. We are welcome to believe in God, Santa Claus, and the Tooth Fairy if we wish. Our ancestors came here to escape religious persecution, and I support every American's right to worship anything or anyone they wish. The problem occurs when these beliefs are forced on society, stunting scientific progress, and extending human suffering. Until we have evidence of a supernatural force that will solve our problems, science is our best hope of eliminating or at least reducing sickness and misery.

The religious extremists will always lose in the end because they're operating from a playbook of first century, symbolic literature worshipped as factual history and supernatural prophecy. The problem is these evidence-less, emotionally-driven beliefs have infected leaders at the highest level of government and are now impeding vital, life-saving scientific research. Supernatural worship should be done in a church or temple, not in Washington. Millions of Americans have died or are still suffering needlessly due to our inability to separate our religious beliefs from our public policy. Is this what you'd expect from a country that boasts of exceptionalism?

Eventually embryonic stem cell research will be fully funded and embraced by both the government and the private sector, which will most likely yield phenomenal results. The good news is more progressive countries have not waited for this to happen and are moving ahead gallantly. The sad news is America is the richest country in the world, and we have the resources to make this happen faster than any other nation. The premise of the religious argument is simple: they, including the Pope, say that human life begins at conception. This is untrue. Until the protoplasm is living and breathing independently it is still only a part of another human being and not an entity in itself. This is a statement based in logical fact, devoid of emotion. This is why abortion is legal in America. A fetus is not a human being and cannot survive without a host. It is simply feeding off of a woman's body, and that woman should have the right to allow that to happen or not. I'm a pro-lifer, but not in the promotional context in which it's presented to the public. I'm all for life, but a fetus is not a human life; it's only a potential human life.

Once it's born it has rights. Before birth, decisions for this non-entity should be left to the woman who created it and is currently hosting it. Only she should be able to decide whether it will become a human being. Unfortunately, the emotionally-charged, faith-based philosophy goes all the way up to the Pope. This is what Pope John Paul II said:

"Human embryos obtained in vitro are human beings and are subjects with rights; and the right to life must be respected from the first moment of their existence."

And there it is. Fertilized eggs classified as human beings by another world leader with no scientific background whose entire platform rests on a 2,000-year-old book. Does this resemble any level of critical thought? Obviously not, and this is what makes organized religion and its leaders so dangerous. Luckily, the scientific community has forged ahead and eventually won nearly every battle along the way, despite years of irrational interference from organized religion. Without these hard fought victories, we would still be living in the Dark Ages.

Reducing human suffering should be our ultimate goal, and embryonic stem cell research has enormous potential to help make that happen. It's just a matter of time before critical thinking outlasts wishful thinking, and sick people get the help they so desperately need. Religious zealots will fight it all the way and delay our progress, but they will eventually lose out to logic, reason, and human decency.

"Religious extremists say that only God has the right to terminate life. Once again, they are speaking for a God for which no proof exists. They would rather protect a dead embryo than offer a cure to millions of suffering human beings who are alive and breathing."

CRITICAL THINKING QUESTION

Is a dead embryo more important than a living human being?

RECOMMENDED RESOURCE

The Stem Cell Hope: How Stem Cell Medicine Can Change Our Lives, by Alice Park

FOREIGN OCCUPATION

Should the United States of America be the policeman of the world? Do we have the right to occupy foreign lands with military forces? The United States currently has troops in 135 countries with 900 military bases, and we justify their presence in a multitude of ways. Not only is it a question of right or wrong, but also one of money. We are broke. If the Federal Reserve couldn't print money, we'd be defaulting on loans across the world. Thanks to wars we didn't need to fight, and money we didn't have to spend, the government has so mismanaged our wealth that we are struggling for our very survival. We are 15 trillion dollars in debt, with no viable solution for solvency. We can't even secure our own borders much less maintain our military might overseas. Our foreign occupation strategies were created after World War II, and they continue to increase. The problem is the world has changed, and we are no longer the fiscal powerhouse of the past. The delusional thinking is that we can continue our 21st century strategy without bankrupting the country. Critical thinking says it's time to bring all the troops home, secure our borders like Fort Knox, and reduce our foreign policy to negotiation, trade embargos, and other fiscal restrictions. No country is foolish enough to attempt to invade the United States using traditional military tactics. And with our borders properly secured and heavily guarded, we could all sleep better at night. This strategy would cost a fraction of what we're spending overseas, not to mention the goodwill it would create by allowing other countries to live their own way without U.S. interference. Former President George W. Bush is famous for saying "God wants every country to be free." Have you ever wondered where he got this idea? I know where. He made it up. God didn't have anything to do with it. As much as I love America, I hate the image we've promoted around the globe that we have all the answers and are the standard bearers of the world. For all our claims of "American Exceptionalism," we sure have a lot of problems. I've traveled all over the world, and there's no question that in many ways America is outstanding. That's why I choose to live here. But to imply that we are smarter, more educated, or morally superior to the rest of the world is ridiculous. Yes, we've done a lot of good things. We've also squandered our wealth, imposed our political values and moral code, and invaded countries for oil. In the richest country in the world, 40 million of our citizens live in poverty. We are the world's largest consumer of addictive narcotics and we've stopped producing products other countries want to buy. Washington is bookended by left-wing socialists determined to create a nanny state, and right-wing fundamentalists trying to legislate morality. We've gotten away with this nonsense for years because we were rich and powerful. No one argues with the biggest kid in the class. It's not smart. But that was yesterday and yesterday's gone. The other kids in the class have been working out, saving their money, and getting smarter. The American empire we created against the founders' wishes is unsustainable. Unless we change radically in the next few years, our way of life is in jeopardy. We begin by pulling the troops out of every country we occupy. Next, we secure our borders and beef up our military at home. Then we stop imposing our beliefs, morals, and values on other countries. It's time for us to grow up and realize we're no smarter than anyone else. It's time for America to stop telling the world what to do and start minding its own business. After all, if we're so smart, why are we struggling with so many self-inflicted wounds? Let's get our act together before telling others how to live.

"President George W. Bush is famous for saying 'God wants every country to be free.' Have you ever wondered where he got this idea? I know where. He made it up."

CRITICAL THINKING QUESTION

If you were deeply in debt with no prospect or plan to pay your way out, would you have vacation homes in 135 countries?

RECOMMENDED RESOURCE

A Concise History of U.S. Foreign Policy, by Joyce P. Kaufman

MEDICARE

Americans over 65 have relied on Medicare since 1966, but few realize the trouble this government-run health-care system is in. Medicare is a Ponzi scheme that takes money from people in the workforce and filters it to retired and disabled people. Like any Ponzi scheme, the system works until you begin paying out more than you take in, which is what's happening now. 10,000 baby boomers turn 65 every day in, and this will continue through 2030. With the average life expectancy crowding 80, this means most people will be feeding off of the Medicare system for 15 years. This, combined with the rapidly rising costs of healthcare, will exhaust the Medicare trust fund by 2017. The delusional thinking is that the federal government can continue to operate Medicare under the same guidelines without running a deficit. Medicare is a lifesaving program that needs to be fixed, and the answer is bringing it into the 21st century. Critical thinking demands that we look at how Medicare was created through the lens of objective reality. In 1966, the average American lived to be 70. In 2012, people are living to the age of 80. You don't have to be a mathematician to solve this problem: the retirement age and the age in which you become eligible for Medicare should be raised by 10 years, to age 75. According to the World Health Organization, Americans are not only living longer, we are living more active lives for a longer period of time. Delaying Medicare until age 75 would save the system until the next major leap in life expectancy, when it should be raised again. Opponents of this idea claim it's not fair to seniors who were promised benefits at age 65. This could be solved by grandfathering in people over 50. Would there be a public outcry of unfairness? Of course. That's life. But if we want to save the system without running up trillions in debt we must do something radical. A Band-Aid approach to a problem of this magnitude is foolish. This is serious business, and it's going to require a mentally tough congress to fix it. For many of us, retiring at 65 is a waste. At 65, most of us are still in our prime, and the work force needs our wisdom and experience. If work isn't your thing, save enough money and self-fund your healthcare retirement. After all, America is the easiest place in the world to build wealth. Critical thinking isn't for the faint of heart, but either is facing a future without Medicare, or the prospect of enslaving our grandchildren with debt because we didn't have the discipline to do what was necessary while we had the chance. It's time to get tough and fix the system, and if the current crop in Congress doesn't have the stomach for the job, let's throw them out and elect a new crop. With Medicare, we're running out of time, and as healthcare costs continue to skyrocket, it's going to be a fast decline. The second solution is to put an end to Medicare fraud, which is costing the system 60 billion dollars a year. Being convicted of Medicare fraud should carry a mandatory 50 year sentence. This would be a virtual life sentence for most offenders, which is appropriate considering that their crime is seriously contributing to the destruction of the Medicare system. In September, 2011, Lawrence Duran was sentenced to 50 years in prison for defrauding Medicare of 205 million dollars. This sentence is the longest in Medicare fraud history, the previous record was 30 years. This will deter future criminals, some of whom have told authorities that one of the reasons they were willing to risk being caught was due to light punishment by the state. The new law would make the 50 year sentence mandatory, so criminals would be essentially risking their lives attempting to defraud Medicare. The jails are full of people who have committed victimless crimes, but we're leaving convicted Medicare fraud criminals off easy? How about letting all the convicted drug dealers out of jail and making room for these criminals who are destroying our healthcare safety net? People who sell drugs aren't forcing customers to buy; they're simply supplying a product their customers want. It may not be a smart personal choice, but it is a choice. The American taxpayer is not asking to be ripped off. If we start seriously punishing people for this crime, criminals will think twice about taking a chance. The good news is the 50 year sentence Lawrence Duran is serving has set a precedent, and hopefully it will continue. Saving that 60 billion dollars a year is a good start to solvency. Delusional thinking must end for Medicare to survive without adding trillions to the deficit. The time to act is now.

"In 1966, the average American lived to be 70. In 2012, people are living to the age of 80. You don't have to be a mathematician to solve this problem: the retirement age and the age in which you become eligible for Medicare should be raised by 10 years, to age 75."

CRITICAL THINKING QUESTION

Why not legalize drugs and help fund Medicare with the tax revenues and savings from emptying our jails?

RECOMMENDED RESOURCE

Medicare in Simple Words,
by Mark Coleman

MEDICAID

Medicaid is the sister program to Medicare, designed as a safety net for the disabled and indigent. It's the fourth largest item in the federal budget, costing taxpayers over 300 billion dollars per year. Since the states are also involved in Medicaid funding, the cost is even higher, and typically the states' second largest expenditure. In essence, Medicaid is welfare healthcare and provides medical and long-term care to roughly 15% of the population. With the flood of baby boomers turning 65, and the recent economic crash, Medicaid is being stretched beyond its limits. Add in the exploding cost of healthcare and you have a disaster in the making. 70% of Americans end up on Medicaid, and the with the average life span at nearly 80 years, that's 15 years of feeding off of government funding for survival. Simply stated, the math doesn't work. And this isn't only a federal problem. The state governments bear about 25% of the Medicaid burden, and their budgets were already stretched before the boomers started turning 65. The real threat is the cost of long-term care, especially skilled nursing, which can cost anywhere from 75,000-150,000 dollars per year. The money isn't there, and without excessive borrowing or a total overhaul, the system will collapse. And this is only the economic issue. There's actually another major problem of equal importance: quality of care. This has been an issue since the beginning of the program, but has been dialed back to secondary status due to the ongoing fiscal concerns. Laura Katz Olson, author of *The Politics of Medicaid,* says, "The vital linkages between financial and patient abuse were for the most part ignored from the start. A substantial number of healthcare providers mistreated and neglected their clients. In some jurisdictions, physicians, dentists, and other professionals were seeing as many as 100 patients daily and not providing even minimal care." The delusional thinking promoted and perpetuated by the government is that Medicaid is a safety net, while the evidence clearly shows a history of poor quality care and even abuse. You can't have a safety net without safety.

I never understood the depth of this issue until my dad had to stay in a nursing home for two weeks for rehab. I got to choose the facility, which is a nursing home owned by the country's largest provider. I went on the Medicare gov website and researched the government's ratings: every single facility in our area covered by Dad's PPO had a "Below Average" rating. I met with the facility directors, and they assured me that these ratings were skewed by various criteria not taken into consideration, and since I had about three hours' notice of my dad leaving the hospital, I had to find a facility immediately. I figured with seven family members visiting him every day, no one would dare attempt substandard care. The doctors, nurses, and staff were pleasant during his stay, but I wouldn't recommend any of them to someone used to world-class care. In their defense, they are understaffed and probably underpaid and doing a high stress job. But my dad did mention several times that staff members yelled at him for one thing or another, and it infuriated me and our family. We were getting ready to transfer him to a private five-star facility, but he passed away at the end of the second week. It wasn't the staff's fault at any level; he was very sick and they did the best they could. But I won't ever recommend that anyone enter a facility where the government has issued a one-star rating. In this case, the so called safety net isn't always safe, and the system needs to be fixed. Outside of billions in taxpayer dollars being needed to guarantee quality care in the system, critical thinking says a partial solution is assigning a patient advocate to each nursing home patient who has a need for one. My dad was lucky; his family was watching every move the doctors and staff made. We knew every medication he was taking down to exact doses. But what about the patients with no family or friends? Who serves as their advocate? If you were old, sick, and alone, wouldn't you want someone watching over you? The bottom line is the government is bloated, broke, and not capable of solving problems of this magnitude. Are they trying? Of course. But the only group powerful enough to solve a problem of this magnitude is the American people. On our own, we are strong. Together, we are a force of nature. If we band together we can accomplish anything. Even the monumental task of insuring that we all get the quality healthcare we need, especially as we age, and even if we are indigent or disabled. We need one another to do the jobs the government can't do on its own.

"Medicaid is a safety net, while the evidence clearly

shows a history of poor quality care and even abuse.

You can't have a safety net without safety."

CRITICAL THINKING QUESTION

With a storied history of patient
neglect and abuse, why hasn't the
government created a volunteer-
driven patient advocate program?

RECOMMENDED RESOURCE

The Politics of Medicaid, by
Laura Katz Olson

DEFENSE SPENDING

America invests almost 700 billion dollars per year on the military, which comprises 42% of the world's military spending. China spends the second most with 114 billion dollars per year. Needless to say, the United States military industrial complex is out of control. The last 10 years haven't helped. The simultaneous wars fought in Iraq and Afghanistan cost us nearly a trillion dollars. Defenders of the Department of Defense (DOD) budget claim we must continue to spend to keep the country safe, and besides, the 700 billion dollars is only 4% of America's Gross Domestic Product (GDP). During WW II, military spending was 34% of GDP. The fact is that with advances in technology and weapons systems, the U.S. military of WW II can't be compared to our 21st century military machine. The delusion in this equation is that military spending is the same thing as defense spending. It's not. Congressman and Presidential candidate Ron Paul has championed this idea for years, and he's correct. Just because we spend 700 billion dollars a year on the military doesn't mean it's all being allocated to making us safer. Critical thinking says a lot of it is making us less safe, mostly the money that funds the 900 military bases we have in 135 different countries. Proponents of this strategy say we must maintain this presence in order to protect America's allies and interests. Opponents say we do it because we want to be the policeman of the world. While I agree that we need troops in hotbed areas, 135 countries is overkill, and it's bankrupting us. Not to mention that many of the countries that house our bases resent us and wish we would leave. Imagine the money that could be saved, and the debt we could trim off the deficit if we closed half of these foreign bases and brought the troops home. Wouldn't we be safer and better served if the bases in Japan, Germany, and Saudi Arabia were moved to Texas, Arizona, and New Mexico? How about bringing all of these troops home to guard and protect the U.S. border? After all, doesn't a well-protected border make us safer than a foreign military base? The problem is a big chunk of the defense budget doesn't make us any safer; it simply gives us a dominant presence on foreign soil. Who are we as a country to impose our will on other nations? Who died and made us king? What makes the United States government believe they know better than other governments? It's no wonder so many people around the world hate us and resent our intrusion. President Obama's defense secretary, Leon Panetta, claims that any cuts in military spending will result in another 1% hike in unemployment, which at the time of this writing is 8%. But studies show that part of the money saved by trimming military spending could be reinvested in education that would create more than twice the jobs as it does in the military. Secretary Panetta knows this, but most of the public doesn't. Instead of being forthright and honest with people, the president and defense secretary want to scare them into believing we are less safe if we make any cuts in the DOD budget. Admiral Mike Mullen summed it up best on when he said on Fox News, "The biggest threat to our national security is the deficit." Other experts have publicly stated that our military threats around the world would recede if we left some of these countries. The bottom line is the government loves power, and America is moving from an exceptional country to an empire. We all know the history of empires, which is one of greed and eventual failure. The United States cannot afford to occupy the world, and it's time we stopped pretending that all military spending is contributing to our defense. With a 15 trillion dollar debt, a substantial portion of which is being underwritten by China, we need to make serious cuts in military spending and reduce the deficit. With healthcare costs exploding and Social Security paying out more than it's taking in, we need the money to make sure Medicare, Medicaid, and Social Security survive. It's time we demand that Washington start using unemotional critical thinking to gain control of this burgeoning, bloated, beast.

"The problem is a big chunk of the defense budget doesn't make us any safer; it simply gives us a dominant presence on foreign soil. Who are we as a country to impose our will on other nations? Who died and made us king?"

CRITICAL THINKING QUESTION

Shouldn't our defense dollars be spent on defense instead of foreign occupation?

RECOMMENDED RESOURCE

Budgeting for Hard Power: Defense and Security Spending Under Barack Obama, by Michael E. O'Hanlon

THE FEDERAL RESERVE

The Federal Reserve was created by Congress in 1913 in order to stabilize the business cycle, control inflation, maintain a solvent banking system, and regulate the financial system. There are no limits on the number of dollars the government and the Fed can print. The Fed has the unique ability to print money on demand. This enables the United States government to fund wars, create bailouts, and spend money like a drunken sailor with absolutely no obligation to pay it back. The money the Fed prints has nothing but good faith behind it. Since President Richard Nixon abandoned the gold standard in 1971, there is no tangible asset to back up the fiat currency. This allows the government to live well beyond its means, passing the debt along to our children and grandchildren. The delusion among the American populous is that the Fed is there to protect us from insolvency, when the truth is it's the Fed itself that's responsible for creating sharp declines in the economy. The banking industry loves the Fed because it allows them to take massive risks, through fractional reserve banking, (where the bank only has a fraction of the money they've taken in on hand) reap huge profits when times are good, and get rescued

★   ★   ★   ★   ★   ★   **137**

when times are bad. It's a no lose situation for the banks. Hans Sennholz, author of Money and Freedom, calls the creation of the Fed "the most tragic blunder ever committed by Congress. The day it was passed, old America died and a new era began." The Fed is a public-private partnership, a coalition of large banks that are the owners working with the approval of the government, which appoints its managers. The craziest part is the government has essentially no oversight. The government can't even audit the Fed. This absolute power has led to supersized corruption and organizational abuse the scope of which most citizens can't even comprehend. The Fed's unlimited ability to print money with no accountability is like issuing a teenager a credit card with no limit. This is probably a little insulting to most teenagers, many of whom would have enough common sense (or guilt) to stop spending at some point. The Fed seems to harbor no such guilt. The massive bailout in 2009 was a complete disaster. The Fed gave billions to the banks with the idea that they would stimulate the economy by loaning the money to their customers, but the banks were not obligated to do so. So they didn't. They simply sat on the money and watched businesses go bankrupt, with no oversight or interjection from the government. When comedian Bill Maher interviewed the chairman of the House Oversight and Government Reform Committee and asked her where the 700 billion dollars went, she said she "didn't know."

Maverick Congressman Dr. Ron Paul, (R-Texas) in his book, End the Fed says, "Deficit spending is a scheme for the confiscation of wealth." Critical thinking backs up what Congressman Paul says. Simply stated, when the Fed creates inflation by printing more money into circulation, the value of the dollar goes down and robs people of their savings. And the average American citizen has no idea he's being systematically robbed by an organization endorsed by the United States government. The average citizen doesn't understand what the Federal Reserve does, much less the negative impact it has on their financial lives. It's time for Americans to educate themselves, stand up and demand massive reform or complete abolishment of the Fed. Until then, this unregulated, misunderstood money manipulating machine will continue to control the world.

"The Feds unlimited ability to print money with no accountability is like issuing a teenager a credit card with no limit."

CRITICAL THINKING QUESTION

If America is truly a free market economy, how can we justify the existence of the Federal Reserve?

RECOMMENDED RESOURCE

End The Fed, by Ron Paul

WAR ON DRUGS

The war on drugs has been a colossal failure since its inception during the Nixon administration. The delusional thinking is obvious and embarrassing, yet the United States government continues spending billions every year trying to stop Americans from getting high. Apparently we're so stupid we must be saved from ourselves. It's astonishing that for 236 years Americans were smart enough to change the world through innovation, technology, and independent thinking, yet our own government doesn't believe we're smart enough to manage our own lives. Didn't we learn this lesson during prohibition? The 19th Amendment outlawing alcohol was as big a failure as the drug war, the only difference is we repealed prohibition after 12 years. Where is the critical thinking in believing the drug war would be any different? After all, isn't alcohol a liquid drug? Marijuana creates a softer effect than alcohol, yet our jails are full of people who like to use and sell it. The drug war philosophy is a zero-sum equation, which is, who owns our bodies? If you say the United States government owns our bodies, that would give them the right to ban substances that harm us. But I don't think anyone would say the government owns our bodies. So if we own our bodies, shouldn't we have the right to drink, smoke, or ingest anything we choose? Who are we hurting by using drugs other than ourselves? Make no mistake: the drug war hasn't stopped Americans from doing drugs. You can buy any drug in any city in America by simply approaching a few people. The drug war has made the drug trade so profitable that damn near everyone is in the business. Finding a drug dealer is easier than buying beer at 7-Eleven, and they don't even ask for ID. Most people who do drugs are casual users who still get up for work every day and live responsibly. Only a small percentage of people become addicts, just as only a small percentage of people become alcoholics. Instead of spending billions of dollars pretending they can squelch demand, the government should legalize drugs and invest a tiny fraction of the savings in educating people on the dangers of drugs and helping the addicted. Not only would legalization save billions and empty half of our jails, it would also save tens of thousands of lives around the world from the vicious drug cartels. According to CBS News, 47,500 people were killed by drug cartels in Mexico between 2007 and 2012. And that's only in one country. Critical thinking says if you remove the profit you remove the violence, but logic and reason don't always prevail in America. The moral police do. These are people who believe they know how to run our lives better than we do, and they are here to save us from ourselves. These crusaders believe they are morally and intellectually superior, and they have blessed us with their presence so we too can see the light. These are the same clowns who can't balance the budget or stop themselves from emailing lewd pictures to college girls, but... they are here to guide us. What a joke. Here's my critical thinking solution: get out of our lives. We own our bodies, and in a so-called free society we have the right to use them as we please, as long as we're not hurting anyone else in the process. If I get high on heroin, that's my problem. If I get high on heroin and hurt someone, I go to jail. The people that say hard drugs cannot be legalized are kidding themselves. Millions of Americans are using them every day. The only logical solution is to stop spending money trying to slow them down. It isn't right and it doesn't work. I'm not advocating drug use. Drugs scare me. What I'm suggesting is applying critical thinking to an issue where none exists. The government should use our tax money to protect us, not to tell us how to live. Just the fact that alcohol is legal but marijuana isn't is proof of how screwed up our legal system is. I mean really, how can we justify one and not the other? Have you ever smoked pot? All it does is put you to sleep. Alcohol, on the other hand, is rough stuff. If alcohol and marijuana were animals, alcohol would be an anaconda and pot would be a pussycat. Yet pot will land you in jail but you can drink alcohol in the White House. The big controversy now is medical marijuana.

So let me get this straight: there are sick people who feel better smoking pot, and we have to debate whether or not they can have access to it? Some cancer patient feels nausea from chemotherapy, smokes pot to get through it, and we throw him in jail? Where is the morality in that? Where are all the religious leaders on this one? It's inconceivable that in 21st century America we're still having these child-like debates. How about we take the money we save from legalizing pot and give some poor guy as much as he wants so maybe he can sleep through the night? To score points with the public, politicians love to claim that America is a Christian nation founded on Christian values. But if they really believed that would they allow our cancer patient to suffer by denying him medical marijuana? What would Jesus do? Would he deny relief to this suffering man or would he pass him a joint? Is allowing someone to suffer for the sake of suffering moral? In some ways America is advanced, and in others our society is the emotional equivalent of a spoiled teenager. This is why critical thinking rooted in logic and reason must replace delusional thinking based in emotion before it's too late.

"According to CBS News, 47,500 people were killed by drug cartels in Mexico between 2007 and 2012. And that's only in one country. Critical thinking says if you remove the profit you remove the violence, but logic and reason don't always prevail in America. The moral police do."

CRITICAL THINKING QUESTION

The drug war has lasted twice as long as prohibition and has failed on every level. How long will we keep repeating the same strategy and expecting a different result?

RECOMMENDED RESOURCE

No Price Too High: Victimless Crimes and the Ninth Amendment, by Robert M. Hardaway

GAMBLING

According to Harvard University Magazine, over 81% of Americans have gambled at some point in their lives. Gross revenues for gambling in America are nearly 100 billion dollars per year. That's more money than Americans spend on sports events, movies, and video games combined. You might even say that without gambling revenues to subsidize the American Revolution, the United States would still be under British rule. Throughout our 236 year history, we've used gambling as a revenue producing strategy. Instead of raising taxes, we've collected billions of dollars giving people what they want: the thrill of betting. Gambling is another stunning example of delusional thinking and moral hypocrisy. Let's examine the equation and look for logic: America is home to Las Vegas, the gambling Mecca of the western world. People travel from every part of the globe to experience the thrill of chance and witness the obnoxious wealth it creates. Billions of dollars in revenue are generated every year from Las Vegas to Atlantic City, yet gambling in most places is illegal. The U.S. Government has reached the conclusion that gambling is only a good thing in certain areas, or more specifically, that only certain types of gambling are appropriate in certain areas. The government claims that laws against gambling are designed to protect us. The question is, protect us from whom? The U.S. government is one of the most inefficient, incompetent organizations in the country, and they're posing as our protectors? 100 million dollars is spent every day in legal casinos across the country, yet in most places, gambling is illegal. Playing the lottery is legal, and a significant number of the people who play it are poor. The Government earns as much as 50% profit from the lottery, which is higher than most casinos. The New York lottery raises more than 2 billion dollars in annual revenue, which is roughly 5% of the state's education budget. Yearly revenue produced by Las Vegas casinos is upward of 12 billion dollars. According to the National Gambling Impact Study Commission, (NGISC) about 125 million Americans gamble. The NGISC estimates that approximately 7.5 million are problem gamblers. They define a problem gambler as one who wages more money than he can afford. Opponents of gambling pose their arguments in three categories: moral, economic, and compulsive. Moral arguments tend to come from religious groups who insist on legislating their brand of morality; a strategy that has been a colossal failure over the course of American history. It's another example of people trying to tell us how to live our lives when in many cases, they can't even manage their own. The economic objection is rooted in the fact that the poor spend 2.5 times more money on gambling than the rich or middle class, which drives some opponents of legalization to claim that gambling is taking advantage of the poor. This is a prime example of America's nanny-state mentality, where the government is supposed to be responsible for citizen's decisions. If the poor are foolish enough to gamble away their money, whose fault is it? These people are poor, not stupid. They're adults, not children. Thomas Jefferson once said, "The lottery is the ideal fiscal instrument, exacting payment solely from those who choose to play." That statement by the author of the Declaration of Independence sums up what America is all about: freedom of choice. Whether you're rich, middle class or poor, you should have the right to choose. George Will, the celebrated American writer said, "Gambling is as American as the state lotteries that helped fund the Revolution." The last concern is compulsive gambling, which some say is an addiction akin to alcohol or drugs. As well-intentioned as gambling critics may be, who are they to tell us how to spend our money? Are we really so pathetic that we can't make our own decisions, manage our own mistakes, and cope with the consequences? America is a free country, but as long as government restricts us from living on our own terms, we remain slaves to elected officials. Historical data suggests that whether it's legal or not, people are going to gamble. Instead of continuing our Don Quixote policy of partial prohibition, let's legalize it across the board and collect billions in taxes. With a fifteen trillion dollar national debt, (and climbing) we need the money. Yearly taxes on poker alone would generate 10-42 billion dollars per year. That's money we could use to reduce the deficit, rebuild our aging infrastructure, and protect our borders. Instead, we simply inflate the currency by asking the Federal Reserve to print more money with no way to pay it back. How moral is it that with every billion-dollar bailout another generation of unborn Americans will be strangled with their grandparents' debt? Here's my critical thinking solution: Grow up, America, and get out of the morality business.

"The lottery is the ideal fiscal instrument,

exacting payment solely from those who

choose to play." — Thomas Jefferson

CRITICAL THINKING QUESTION

Why not leave the moral issue of gambling to the adults that choose to engage in it, and legalize it in every state to raise revenue?

RECOMMENDED RESOURCE

Legalized Gambling: Revenue Boom or Social Bust? by Matt Doeden

★   ★   ★   ★   ★   ★

PHARMACEUTICAL INDUSTRY

The pharmaceutical business is among the most demonized in America. The premise is that it's an evil empire that overcharges for lifesaving drugs we need to survive. This is another example of mass delusion. The pharmaceutical industry invests billions of dollars each year in research and development never knowing whether they will even recoup their costs. The approximate expenditure of bringing a drug from discovery to market is around 1.3 billion dollars, and that's just for the first pill. That only includes drugs that make it through a number of clinical trials, and the rigorous FDA approval process, which includes four exhaustive phases that take an average of eight years to complete. Even when a manufacturer develops a successful drug, the company only has the exclusive rights to its own patent for 17 years, which is when the United States government overreaches into the industry and forces manufacturers to reveal their proprietary formula for competitors to copy. This is one of the ways politics enters into this industry, and why I've included it in this section. Why should the government have the right to steal the intellectual property of a private or public corporation in a free market? The answer is they don't, unless America is not truly a free market. The fact is the government abuses its power when it determines it's in the best interest of the country. This is clearly not what the founders intended, but you'll find little public resistance to this larceny, and that's how they get away with it. Its socialism masked as fair practice. This is one of the problems with our government: the more successful you become the more interest the looters in Washington have in your business. America was built on the entrepreneurial spirit of hard work, risk, and reward. It's what made us the economic wonder of the world. But in recent years there's been a gradual shift toward the socialistic philosophy that says once you reach a certain level of success you are morally obligated to become your brother's keeper. Few industries have taken the necessary risks and achieved the success of the pharmaceuticals, and as a reward for employing hundreds of thousands of people and bankrolling cutting edge scientific research, they are criticized and villainized. With total U.S. sales of nearly 900 billion dollars per year, this is a level of success too great for the government to resist over-regulating. Until someone in power gets sick...in which time the evil empire who creates the lifesaving drugs becomes their best friend. One veteran sales rep confided to me during a ride along, "It's not a case of biting the hand that feeds us, but of biting the hand that saves our very lives. It's a childish mentality." I find it slightly peculiar that we celebrate the troops who protect us, but villainize the people who discover and distribute the medications that save us. Maybe we should be thanking them for their service? I have and will continue to do so. Would we be happier if pharmaceutical companies and doctors were poor? Where would the money come from to attract the best medical minds to practice medicine and develop new cures to old diseases? We should be celebrating these people instead of over-regulating, fining, and threatening them with career ending malpractice suits. The claims of price gouging by the drug companies are also unfounded. The only way to guarantee companies long term survival is to charge fair market prices for their products. As in any industry competing in a free market, a drug company overcharging for their products would quickly be eliminated by its competitors.

As a speaker, trainer, and consultant to some of the largest pharmaceutical companies, I can tell you from first-hand experience that no one works harder and is more dedicated to saving and extending lives than the men and women of this amazing industry. In spite of enduring endless criticism from the media and general public, these people forge ahead knowing they are making a massive difference in people's lives and in the world at large. Martha Reid, a senior executive for the past 23 years at one of the world's largest, most successful pharmaceutical companies says, "We're on a mission to improve global health. It's about having an impact on diseases that affect not only large numbers of people, but also small numbers of people that would be overlooked if we didn't have the discretionary research and development money to invest. If we take profit out of the equation, drug discovery on its current scale will stop." This is critical thinking from an industry insider.

What the public doesn't see are all the failed attempts that drug manufacturers must absorb as a cost of doing business. 80% of drugs never prove safe and effective enough to make it to market, and manufacturers must offset these massive losses with the 20% that succeed. This is a statistic you won't hear much in the media or around the water cooler. It's easier to criticize an industry than educate yourself about it. If you kill the profits these companies earn, they will be forced to back out of research projects and lay off scientists who are on the verge of major medical breakthroughs. After working with thousands of pharmaceutical sales reps, managers, and executives, I can assure you that these people are in this business much more as a mission than for money. Do they make a good living? You bet, and they should. I've gone with them on sales calls all over the country, and in my opinion, they are underpaid. The fact is the drug reps know just as much about their drugs as the doctors who prescribe them. Few salespeople have the talent and tenacity to perform this service. The money they earn is well deserved. The managers and senior executives are just as hard working and dedicated, and being on the front line in this industry is no picnic. "The sales reps sell their products under a very strict regulatory and legal environment," claims Reid. Only after months of product and disease-state training are they allowed to engage a doctor or healthcare professional in a clinical discussion related to their product. No product gets used in this country without the medical decision of a physician."

The demonization of this industry is part of a growing philosophy in America that discriminates against the rich and successful. The Obama administration has taken this warped philosophy to new heights, and unless critical thought prevails, the America we love will cease to exist. The idea that big corporations, profitable industries, and rich citizens should be demonized, overtaxed, and punished will lead to a mass exodus of producers and job creators that Ayn Rand wrote about in her brilliant 1957 novel, Atlas Shrugged. America's very survival depends on our ability to stop thinking emotionally and start thinking critically. In the absence of this cultural shift, we are doomed to become a socialistic, welfare, food stamp state.

"We're on a mission to improve global health. It's about having an impact on diseases that affect not only large numbers of people, but also small numbers of people that would be overlooked if we didn't have the discretionary research and development money to invest. If we take profit out of the equation, drug discovery on its current scale will stop." — Martha Reid, pharmaceutical executive

CRITICAL THINKING QUESTION

If pharmaceutical companies create drugs that save, extend and improve our lives, why do we insist on demonizing them?

RECOMMENDED RESOURCE

Shaping the Industrial Century: The Remarkable Story of the Evolution of the Modern Chemical and Pharmaceutical Industries (Harvard Studies in Business History) by Alfred Dupont Chandler

ASSISTED SUICIDE

A few months ago our beloved 12-year-old dachshund, Robin the rat dog, was diagnosed with cancer. The veterinarian recommended we euthanize her immediately to relieve the excruciating pain. As heartbreaking as it was, we decided it was the best thing to do for our little buddy. After all, no one would allow their cherished pet to suffer. Americans love their pets, and many of us have experienced this heartbreaking scenario. It's not pleasant, but it is the right thing to do. For animals it's legal; for human beings, it's murder. Exceptions are the states of Oregon, Washington, and Montana. And these three state laws are under the constant threat of being overturned. So faced with terminal illness and significant suffering, we don't even have the legal right to end our pain. For animals it's humane; for humans it's a capital offense. We refuse to allow animals to suffer yet we are committed to making sure people die naturally no matter how much misery they must endure. Heroes like the late Dr. Jack Kevorkian were villainized and thrown in jail for helping people escape their suffering. The delusion is we don't own our own bodies and lives. Critical thinking says that people should have 100% control over their own decisions as long as those decisions don't violate the rights of others. This is fourth-grade logic our elected officials are apparently incapable of comprehending.

Dr. Kevorkian had the moral courage to answer the desperate pleas of the terminally ill and was subsequently rewarded with an eight-year jail sentence. In the Roman Catholic Church, suicide is a sin because only God has the authority to end a human life. No evidence exists to support this claim, yet it's the undercurrent of the laws banning assisted suicide. The Christian Apologetics and Research Ministry (CARM) says this: "God is the sovereign Lord who determines the day we die. Therefore, we are not to undermine God's authority." Once again we have religious leaders and organizations telling us what God wants with no proof to support their statements. Make no mistake: this is not about what God wants. This is religious zealotry masquerading as morality. This is about controlling society, and it works on the masses. The problem is, once critical thinking is injected into the equation this mass manipulation becomes obvious. The Catholic Church, one of the most powerful organizations in human history, has this to say about someone who decides to end their life of suffering: "The patient seriously damages his relationship with God." Here's my critical thinking question on this bold statement from the Catholic Church: "How do they know?" The Church, Catholic or any other, has no more information than you or I do. Years ago they did, and that's where the manipulation began. People didn't have access to information and were largely ignorant and terrified to challenge the Church. Those days are gone. Today Americans are armed with more information and education at their fingertips than all the generations that preceded us combined. It's easy to scare an uneducated, ignorant populous, but once the playing field of education, knowledge, and awareness is leveled, everything changes. Educated people cannot be bullied or brainwashed. In the information age, you'd better have extraordinary evidence to support extraordinary claims, and religion offers no such evidence. The religious right's case against assisted suicide is based on a book written by relatively ignorant men. Today's 12-year-old knows more about the world than the greatest scholars of the Iron Age and the authors of the Bible. The leap of faith that Christianity demands is that the Bible was inspired, and therefore written, by God Himself. Again, not a shred of evidence exists to prove this claim. If I told you that the book you're reading was inspired by God, you would immediately marginalize me and consider me a crackpot, and you would be right to do so. Yet religious leaders have no more evidence to support their claim of divine inspiration of their book than I do of mine. Their claim has convinced two billion otherwise intelligent people that their book was written by a supernatural, omniscient being, even though it is filled with first-century ignorance and barbarianism.

They persuade people to willfully abandon critical thought and analysis in exchange for eternal life. I don't offer that with my book, so they have a serious advantage. Once this deal of blind faith for eternal life is struck, religious leaders can say almost anything, and their flock must follow. The idea that a merciful God is against ending human suffering is a prime example. It defies even a child's logic, yet it's ferociously observed and defiantly defended by most Americans. Here's what one religious website had to say about assisted suicide: "God cares about those who are crying out for death to end their suffering. God gives purpose to life even to the end. Only God knows what is best, and His timing is perfect." Maybe they should tell that to the six million Jews who died in the Holocaust. How perfect was God's timing on that one? How about the people who were jumping out of the windows at the World Trade Center during 9/11? And let's not forget the nursery school kids who were instantly incinerated in the Oklahoma City bombing. I'll leave out the other 10,000 examples of merciless atrocities that any God worth worshipping could have easily prevented. Would you allow your children to be slaughtered?

It's time for thinking people to stand up and start

pushing back on issues that involve human suffering. If someone chooses to believe that God wants him/her to suffer through a terminal illness, that's his or her decision, but when you force the rest of us to obey laws based on beliefs without proof, it's wrong and needs to be stopped. You're welcome to believe in Santa Claus, but when you outlaw burning wood in my fireplace so he can slide down the chimney, you're going to have to prove he actually exists. Your faith is yours, not anyone else's. Forcing critical thinkers to adhere to laws based on fairy tales is wrong.

Unfortunately, the Church isn't the only powerful group of people protesting assisted suicide. There are many physicians who are banding together to fight physician-assisted suicide as well. Once again, here's another powerful group of people who used to have far more clout in society than they have now, due to education and information available to the masses. Critical thinking on this is simple: if a physician-assisted suicide violates the individual physician's belief system, he shouldn't be forced to perform this service. For physicians who believe it's the right thing to do, they should be able to do it. This whole argument boils down to a simple premise: who is in charge of our lives? Doctors? Politicians? Religious leaders? Or us? Are we so feeble-minded that we cannot be trusted to be responsible for our own existence?

The answer is obviously no, yet that's exactly what the people in power would have us believe. They brainwash us to believe we need their laws, dogma, and leadership to live our lives so they can exert their control. When will Americans grow up emotionally and accept the fact that this is the one and only life we have evidence of that exists, and we should be allowed to live it on our own terms? A few months ago, as my father lay dying in a south Florida hospital, my wife mentioned that she would be willing to slip my dad some pills to end his life if his pain became unbearable. As much as it shocked me, I thought it might be a viable option if his condition worsened, and he requested it. Of course, if we were caught, we would be jailed for manslaughter. This is further evidence of the emotional immaturity of American society, and the root of the problem is our insistence on forcing our puritanical beliefs on others to the point where politicians are pressured to create and pass laws without logic. Luckily, there are thousands of critical thinking American citizens who are committed to ending these laws. Derek Humphry, the founder of the Hemlock Society and author of the million copy best seller Final Exit, is one of the leading proponents of the fight to legalize assisted suicide. After seeing his wife suffer and answering her pleas for relief, he helped her end a life of misery in 1975. Humphry has served as the movement's greatest champion ever since. Compassion and Choices, based in Denver, is also on the cutting edge of this cause.

The states have the power to allow and regulate assisted suicide or to prohibit it, and with enough pressure from critical thinkers we will someday have the freedom to end our lives with dignity. If enough critical thinkers band together, someday we'll be able to live and die on your own terms.

"It's time for thinking people to stand up and start pushing back on issues that involve human suffering. If someone chooses to believe that God wants him to suffer through a terminal illness, that's his decision, but when you force the rest of us to obey laws based on beliefs without proof, it's wrong and needs to be stopped. You're welcome to believe in Santa Claus, but when you outlaw burning wood in my fireplace so he can slide down the chimney, you're going to have to prove he actually exists"

CRITICAL THINKING QUESTION

What right does the government have to force us to suffer in our own bodies?

RECOMMENDED RESOURCE

Final Exit: The Practicalities of Self-Deliverance and Assisted Suicide for the Dying, by Derek Humphry

GUN CONTROL

Gun control has always been a controversial subject in America, but it shouldn't be. The second Amendment clearly states we have the right to bear arms. The founders were clear on this: George Washington said, "A free people ought not only be armed and disciplined, but they should have sufficient arms and ammunition to maintain a status of independence from any who might attempt to abuse them, which would include their own government." This is not surprising given the founders independent spirit and inherent mistrust of government after living under the crown. Firearms are the ultimate leveling of the playing field. Washington also said: "The very atmosphere of firearms anywhere and everywhere restrains evil. They deserve a place of honor with all that is good." Our first president was clearly pro-gun. Thomas Jefferson said this about the gun control laws of his generation: "They disarm only those who are neither inclined nor determined to commit crimes. Such laws make things worse for the assaulted and better for the assailants." This is from the man who penned the Declaration of Independence. No one would ever accuse Jefferson of being a war monger. If there was a pacifist among the founders, it was Jefferson.

But his logic is hard to dispute, and has nothing to do with the fact he said this over 200 years ago. Human nature hasn't changed. Bad people will always have guns and good people should have the right to protect themselves. Banning guns only punishes the innocent and leaves them unable to fight back. Even Gandhi agreed when he said: "Among the many misdeeds of British rule in India, history will look upon the act of depriving a whole nation of arms as the blackest." And this came from the mouth of the man who pioneered non-violent resistance! The only people who win when gun control laws are enacted are the criminals. All these laws do is motivate robbers, muggers, and thieves. The world has a long history of leaders banning firearms for the purpose of weakening the public resistance. Psychopaths like Hitler, Stalin, and Chairman Mao all disarmed their citizens before they destroyed them. It's the old saying about absolute power corrupting absolutely. A gun-toting public evens things out, and that's why guns should stay legal and readily available. The delusion is rooted in linear thinking that leads people to believe banning guns reduces violence and crime. This has been tried again and again and always fails. In 1996, Australia publically destroyed over 600,000 firearms in an attempt at gun control. In 1997, armed robberies in Australia increased by 44%. Critical thinking suggests that reducing violent crime requires a non-linear solution, which starts with firearms training, education, and stricter laws for criminals who use guns and fewer laws for people who fire in self-defense. If a burglar enters your home, you should be able to shoot first and ask questions later. A few weeks ago, a 20-year-old single mother sat in her home holding her baby in one arm and a gun in the other while an armed robber was attempting to break in. Knowing she could be charged with murder if she killed him, she called 911 and asked the operator if it was okay to shoot him. The police were on their way, but she knew they wouldn't make it in time. The robber finally broke in the house and she shot him dead. While this was illegal in her state, no charges have been filed. What jury in their right mind would convict this woman of anything outside of heroism? Someone brandishing a weapon was threatening her life and child, and luckily she was armed and calm enough to pull the trigger. The real question is why did she have to call 911 and ask for permission to defend her life? It's ridiculous. The current gun laws in some states protect the criminals more than the victims. Here's the result of the U.S. National Crime Survey: "If a robbery victim does not defend himself, the robbery will succeed 88% of the time, and the victim will be injured 25% of the time. If the victim resists with a gun, the robbery's success rate falls to 30%, and the injury rate falls to 17%." As congressman and presidential candidate Ron Paul says, "The ultimate protection must come from the individual." And unless you're a karate expert or samurai warrior, protection means firearms. Famous comedian Chris Rock jokes, "If you've got a gun, you don't have to workout!" Funny words from a funny man, but if you're life or property is being threatened, there's nothing funny about it. Actor James Earl Jones, most famous for his role as Darth Vader, says, "The world is filled with violence. Because criminals carry guns, we decent law-abiding citizens should also have guns otherwise they will win and decent people will lose." And that's coming from a Hollywood actor, many of whom have spoken out against guns. Of course many of these anti-gun crusaders travel with bodyguards and live behind gated walls. Are the rest of us supposed to defend ourselves with butter knives and Bible prayers? Criminals prefer an unarmed public, and that's why everyone should consider gun ownership. Sheriff Chuck Wright, of Spartanburg, South Carolina, says "Don't be so naïve to believe the police can be everywhere." And in America, isn't it each citizens responsibility to be our own first line of defense? This belief is reflected in a recent Gallup Poll which reported that 74% of Americans believe they should be able to carry a handgun. These numbers have gone up year after year. According the National Rifle Association, over 100 million Americans own guns. That's roughly one third of the population. Maybe we should be advertising that statistic in the media to warn off would-be robbers. "More guns equals less crime," claims rock star and gun advocate

Ted Nugent, and that's the bottom line. In a perfect world we wouldn't need guns. But until that happens, critical thinking suggests that we all exercise our second amendment rights, voice our support, and keep a close eye on anti-gun crusaders who want to make our decisions for us. Gun ownership is not only practical, it's our constitutional right.

"In 1996, Australia publically destroyed over 600,000 firearms in an attempt at gun control. In 1997, armed robberies in Australia increased by 44%."

CRITICAL THINKING QUESTION

Shouldn't every American have the right to self-protection?

RECOMMENDED RESOURCE

More Guns, Less Crime: Understanding Crime and Gun Control Laws, Third Edition (Studies in Law and Economics), by John R. Lott

GLOBAL WARMING

In the past 100 years the earth has warmed The question is whether or not the problem is man-made or a natural variation in the climate system. Al Gore says "the earth has a fever," but that doesn't mean the fever is being caused by greenhouse gas emissions. Experts and scientists have been debating this issue for decades. In 1988, the United Nations created the Intergovernmental Panel on Climate Change (IPCC), which has delivered inconclusive results. John Coleman, meteorologist and founder of the Weather Channel, has been a long-time critic of the IPCC. Coleman says, "The only proof of the IPCC hypothesis was the computer model predictions. There is no evidence to support the claim of significant man-made global warming." Many experts agree. On the other side of the argument are scientists who are convinced global warming is the result of carbon dioxide from fossil fuels like oil, gas, and coal, and some believe if we don't reverse it soon, it could be the end of the world. Polls show that fewer people today believe in man-made global warming than they did 10 years ago. Piers Corbyn, founder of the Weather Action Foundation says, "Global Warming is delusional nonsense founded on fraud. The

IPCC should be closed down." No matter which side of the argument you're on, one thing is for certain: In the 24 years of its existence, the IPCC has failed to prove man-made global warming. "I think global warming will turn out to be a disgrace to the scientific community and the environmental movement," says Dr. Richard Lindzen, a prominent physicist at the Massachusetts Institute of Technology. Many experts argue that correlation does not equal causation, in this context referring to the fact that just because the earth's temperature is getting warmer, and we are using more carbon, doesn't mean carbon is the cause. The bottom line is that the evidence is inconclusive. The delusional thinking is that the issue of global warming is about saving the planet. It's clearly not. When you dive deeper into the debate, it becomes glaringly apparent that this is about money, and lots of it. Enough money to take over the world; some experts believe the major proponents of the global warming movement are trying to do just that. One major physicist, who refused to allow us to use his name due to receiving multiple death threats, said, "If you control the carbon, you control the planet." John Coleman calls it "The greatest scam in history." Dr. Richard Lindzen of M.I.T. agrees: "The agenda is raising taxes, money, and gaining control over people's lives." The more you scare them, the faster they will comply. The Bible does it with the threat of damnation while the groupies of global warming are doing it with doomsday scenarios. Nothing moves the masses like fear, and history has proven this. If those seeking control and power can sell two billion people on the philosophy of a book written in the first century with no evidence, anything is possible. Trillions of dollars are at stake, as well as the control over our daily lives. The man at the top of the controversy is Maurice Strong, a former United Nations power broker turned billionaire. His critics say his motive is to use global warming to establish a world government. George Hunt, an environmentalist and former associate of Strong's says, "Global warming is a front to take over the world. It's all about money and power." The premise of the world domination idea is that the people in power want to replace the dollar and every other currency with one world currency. And the people that control the currency will control the world. If this sounds like a science fiction conspiracy theory, think again. All you have to do is observe how much power the Federal Reserve has over the money supply. And many of their actions are unregulated, which is why people like Ron Paul want to abolish the Fed. Countries with their own currency can control their own money supply. If the world only had one currency, 99.9 % of us would be at the mercy of the .1 % in control. It's a scary scenario at best, but it's something all of us must be educated about and aware of. Critical thinking says anytime you want to find the source of corruption, all you have to do is follow the money trail. The more panic the power mongers can create, the more control they accumulate. It doesn't matter if it's man made religion or made up science, as long as there's money to be made or control to acquire, there will always be people willing to lie, cheat, and steal to get it.

"Global warming is a front to take over the world.

It's all about money and power."

— George Hunt, environmentalist

CRITICAL THINKING QUESTION

Are money and power big enough
motivators to drive men to create
mass hysteria and public panic
with false evidence?

RECOMMENDED RESOURCE

The Greatest Hoax: How the Global
Warming Conspiracy Threatens Your
Future, by Senator James Inhofe

SCHOOL BULLYING

Bullying has been a problem since the beginning of time, and probably pre-dates humans beginning in the animal kingdom. Anytime there's a perceived imbalance of power viewed through the eyes of a creature who derives pleasure from others misery, you will have bullying. Almost everyone seems to have a bully story from their school days, and none of these tales is pleasant to hear. I can remember being bullied in grammar school by an older tomboy tough girl who beat up all the boys in the lower grades. It sounds funny now, but you're seven years old, weigh 50 pounds and have to find a new route home every day, it's terrifying. Outside of a few isolated incidents in junior high, the bullies left me alone. I was an athlete training five hours a day before and after school and never really engaged in regular social activities. But like many of us, I witnessed some horrendous bullying by mean kids who picked on the weak and made their lives a living hell. Some kids had it so bad in junior high that I started telling my friends I was starting a "little man's union," which would band together all the smaller, passive, and friendly kids to stand up to the bullies. And the craziest thing happened: the kids took it seriously and inundated me with requests to join the little man's union. What was meant as a joke became an entity, because in a union town like Chicago, these kids understood the concept of leverage through numbers. Most of their parents were in a union. The little man's union (LMU) was formed, and within a few months, we had over 100 members. A member would be threatened by a bully and told to meet outside the bike racks after school. But this time the little guy would show up with 50 other LMU members to greet the bully. This went on for my three years and none of us ever threw a punch. The craziest part is how the bullies reacted to our union: they thought it was hysterical. 50 members would meet one giant bully at the bike racks (where all fights at our school took place) and instead of fighting the bullies, they would break out laughing! Maybe it was because our union wasn't a gang, just a rag-tag group of nice little kids that gathered for protection. After six months, the big tough kids were asking to join and eventually formed what they called the big man's union. The unions became a hallway joke at our school and softened the bullies in a way I never expected. We laughed about it all the way through high school. While this is a nice ending to a bullying story, this occurred back in the '70s, long before the days of bullying by text, instant messaging, and social media. experts agree that today's bullies are more vicious, and their victims are living a tortured existence even committing suicide. This is clearly not a rite of passage scenario. Bullying in the 21st century is a matter of life and death. The statistics are staggering: 160,000 American kids stay home from school on any given day to avoid being bullied. This is not a social issue, it's an epidemic. Glenn Stutzky, a school safety consultant said this on ABC News, "We've allowed a culture of abuse to thrive unchecked in our nation's schools and we're paying for it with the bodies of our children. Suicide is bullying's quiet little secret. It's picking off our kids one at a time." Kids like Jamey Rodemeyer, a 14-year-old high school freshman from Buffalo, NY, are taking to the Internet to cry for help. You can pull them up on YouTube. These kids plead for help. They cry, beg, and even hold up signs screaming out for someone to listen. For Jamey Rodemeyer, it was too late. He had been bullied since fifth grade and couldn't take it anymore. In late 2011, he committed suicide. Unfortunately, this is becoming all too common. The delusional thinking as it relates to bullying is how many teachers, school officials, and religious leaders view this as a natural part of growing up. We have kids killing themselves, hiding out at home and even taking revenge in school shootings, yet it's being reduced by authorities as a part of growing up. I've experienced this first hand. Twenty years ago, I was coaching a 14-year-old star tennis player who attended a private Christian school. One day we were training for a tournament, and he told me a gang of bullies at school had threatened to jump him in the parking lot. Feeling honored that he had confided in me, I went to the school the next day and spoke to the principal. He laughed it off and told me I was overreacting, and my tennis star would be perfectly safe. I was livid because this kid was not prone to exaggeration, and I knew the threat was real. I scolded the principal and chastised him for his un-Christ like behavior as the leader of a Christian school. He told me to get out of his office and never return. The next day I put a baseball bat in the front seat of my car and waited for my protégé to get out of school. He walked out, and a group of kids followed him. I walked over to him, and we got into the car. It was a good thing they didn't call my bluff because I wasn't bluffing. The bullies finally stopped threatening him and turned their terror on some other poor kid. I saw this school principal years later at a fundraiser and I mentioned the incident. He reacted the same way he did originally, and insisted I was the problem. Unfortunately, this delusional response is not uncommon. This is what Dr. Robert Newman, Chairman of the California Christian Coalition, said recently about school bullying: "Bullying is a part of growing up. It's a part of maturing. I hardly think bullying is a real issue in schools." This is serious delusion from a major religious leader. With leaders like this, is it any wonder kids are hiding at home instead of going to school? We're not protecting them or even admitting there's a problem. Glenn Stutzky weighed in on this issue with Barbara Walters: "Kid's see the teachers look over and see the bullying and they come to their door and the teachers shut it. What message does that send the kid who's being bullied? And what message does that send the rest of the kids? What kid is going to go up and help a victim when they see adults close their doors?" With 15-25% of U.S. students being bullied on a regular basis, how can we deny this is a serious problem? If we can't count on our teachers and preachers to protect our children, whom can we trust? The denial goes deeper with religious extremists obsessed with aligning bullying with homosexuality. Here's what Candi Cushman, of Focus on the Family said recently about anti-bullying efforts in schools: "What parents need to be aware of is there are activist groups who want to promote homosexuality to kids because they realize if they can capture the hearts and minds of our children at the earliest ages they will have for all practical purposes won the clash of values that we are currently experiencing." This is a classic example of why the far right religious extremists cannot be taken seriously. Their hatred of homosexuals impairs their judgment. Children are bullied for numerous reasons, including being gay. Does it really matter why? This is a critical issue that requires serious people to solve it. If religious leaders aren't part of the solution, they are part of the problem. Their first century worldview is giving bullies an excuse to hurt innocent children. Critical thinking says it's time to pressure educators, parents, and politicians to work together to end bullying in American schools. They need to stop denying the problem, closing their doors, and spewing their homophobia and start acting like leaders. There's no excuse for 160,000 kids a day cowering in terror. The blame rests on the shoulders of the leaders we trust to keep them safe. Anti-bullying laws need to carry severe punishment and be enforced. Bullies should be banished from schools and sent back to their parents. We owe it to our children to protect them and provide an environment where they can successfully and fearlessly learn and grow.

"This is what Dr. Robert Newman, chairman of the California Christian Coalition, said recently about school bullying: 'Bullying is a part of growing up. It's a part of maturing. I hardly think bullying is a real issue in schools.' This is serious delusion from a major religious leader. With leaders like this, is it any wonder kids are hiding at home instead of going to school?"

CRITICAL THINKING QUESTION

Would the homophobic religious extremists be satisfied to allow all minorities to be bullied, including kids of religious extremists?

RECOMMENDED RESOURCE

Bullying Prevention & Intervention: Realistic Strategies for Schools, by Susan Swearer, Dorothy Espelage and Scott Napolitano

DRINKING AGE

The drinking age debate has been raging in this country for as long as most of us can remember. Maybe the best argument for a national drinking age of 18 is the old adage that if a man is old enough to go to war, he's old enough to have a beer. I agree. The delusion is that 18-year-olds aren't drinking anyway. All the law does is create a minor hurdle for an 18 to 20-year-old, and it's not much of a hurdle. An 18-year-old should have the emotional maturity to drink in moderation, and most probably do. That being said, I know 50-year-olds who don't possess this maturity, so age is not the only variable in this equation. Creating a barrier only makes people want more of what they can't have, and history has proven this time and again. Prohibition doesn't work. How many times does history have to prove this?

Part of the thrill many of us enjoyed as teenagers was doing something taboo and getting away with it. Critical thinking say's if you remove the thrill appeal of illegal drinking you'll reduce the motivation to engage in it to excess. And this is one of the unintended consequences of United States Government's "Uniform Drinking Age

Act," passed by congress in 1984. Even though every state has the right to set its own drinking age, the federal act includes a provision that cuts federal highway funding by 10% to penalize states that choose anything under 21. As a result, all states have maintained the 21-year-old law. According to John McCardell, former president of Middlebury College and current director of Choose Responsibility, "Illegal drinkers are more likely to binge." Binging is defined as consuming five or more drinks, which from what I remember from my college days, was pretty common. McCardell is one of the strongest opponents of the 1984 law. "We have lived through prohibition, and it doesn't work, says McCardell. "Alcohol education is what we need. This law has been an abysmal failure. All it does is push it farther underground." Glynn Birch, president of MADD, (Mothers Against Drunk Driving) strongly disagrees: "The 21 law works," claims Birch. "This law is about drunk driving."

While I respect Mr. Birch's opinion and know his intentions are good, I disagree. Saying that legally prohibiting 18-20 year-olds from drinking is going to stop them from driving drunk is parallel to saying refusing to distribute condoms will stop teenagers from having sex. If life were only that simple. This is wishful thinking, and that's why the law has failed. John McCardell is one of the few critical thinkers who are speaking out against this failed policy, and it's time for more of us to step in and voice our opinions.

I can remember sipping my first beer as a high school freshman and thinking it was the worst thing I ever tasted. My friends felt the same way, but all through high school and college there was beer, liquor, and drugs. Half the fun was beating the system by breaking the law. I'm not condoning this behavior. Alcohol and drugs are dangerous. I'm simply saying its human nature to experiment, and rebellion comes with the territory. Telling an 18-year-old he can't drink is daring him to defy you. The bottom line of this argument, whether you're for or against it, is that it doesn't work. And if 18-year-olds can die in battle, serve on a jury, and elect a president, why can't they have a cocktail? They're either grown up or they're not. It's hypocritical to treat them as adults only when it's convenient. There's no credibility or consistency in this strategy. It's no different than alcohol being legal while pot is not. When was the last time you heard about a stoned-driving accident? It's ridiculous, and it's time we grow up in this country and change these incongruent laws.

It's like trying to outlaw sex among college students; 95% of the kids would be in jail. It's just another example of a law based on the delusion that just because you make something illegal people will comply. Critical thinking, with evidence throughout history, says that people (including 18-year-olds) will always find a way to get what they want, and as long as they aren't hurting anyone else, they are adults and should have that right. To ask them to dodge bullets while treating them like children is disrespectful and wrong. They are either adults or they are not. And if we as a nation decide that an 18-year-old is a child, we need to stop sending them to war. After all, what kind of a country sends a child to war?

"Critical thinking, with evidence throughout history, says that people (including 18-year-olds) will always find a way to get what they want, and as long as they aren't hurting anyone else, they are adults and should have that right. To ask them to dodge bullets while treating them like children is disrespectful and wrong. They are either adults or they are not. And if we as a nation decide that an 18-year-old is a child, we need to stop sending them to war. After all, what kind of a country sends a child to war?"

CRITICAL THINKING QUESTION

Aren't the 18-year-olds today more mature than they were 20 years ago?

RECOMMENDED RESOURCE

Should the Drinking Age Be Lowered?, by Hal Marcovitz

SEAT BELT/HELMET LAWS

A few months ago, I was driving from our summer home in north Georgia to our winter home in Palm Beach and I pulled over to get gas. When I finished, I got back in the car and onto the Florida Turnpike and inched up to the toll booth. Before I could reach around to fasten my seat and pay the toll, a Florida Highway Patrolman approached my window and told me to pull over. He asked me why I'm not wearing a seat belt, and I told him I just got back in the car and wanted to pay the toll first. He told me I was technically already on the road and issued me a ticket for $116.00. Now I'm usually very respectful of law enforcement officers. I admire what they do and value their service. But I was so angry at this obvious abuse of power that I had a few words with this officer. When it became apparent he was about to arrest me, I shut up and took the ticket. This is a classic example of how a law with no logic can be abused. The delusion is that the state has the right to tell any of us that we have to wear a seat belt when the only person at risk is us. Whose life is it, anyway? The law that says that children have to wear a seat belt makes sense, since children are often incapable of making rational decisions in their own self-interest. But adults? This is another attack on our individual freedom and liberty, and any critical thinker can recognize it. If I choose not to fasten my seat belt and am injured as a result, that's my responsibility, not the state's. Who are these politicians to tell us what risks we should take with our own lives? When was the power of the people turned over to politicians?

Nobel Prize winning economist Milton Friedman spoke out against this law before his death in 2006. Quoting 19th century philosopher John Stuart Mill, he said, "The only purpose for which power can be rightfully exercised over any member of a civilized society is to prevent harm to others. His own good, either physical or moral, is not a sufficient warrant." Friedman went on to say,"There's absolutely no way you can justify the imposition of safety requirements on autos and motorcycles to protect the drivers of those vehicles." The United States currently has 30 states that have what they call "Primary Seat Beat Laws," which means you can be pulled over for that of-fense alone.

Motorcycle helmet laws are the same. I've had motor-cycles for 35 years and I've almost always worn a helmet. It's a percentage play. If you ride long enough, you will fall or be hit by something. It's inevitable. Especially when you have drivers texting. But to force motorcyclists to wear a helmet for their own good is another infringement on our civil liberties. Here's the critical thinking message to our state legislators: Get out of our lives! You can't even run your own lives, so what makes you think you can run ours? More importantly, you have no right. The bottom line of these two laws is that the consequences of breaking them only impacts the disobedient individual. If I smash my skull on the street because I chose not to wear a helmet, it's my skull to crush. Treating adults like children is unacceptable, and when enough critical thinkers rise up and fight these foolish laws, they will change. The argument that the unintended consequences of my negligence creates an additional financial burden on society through my hospitalization and subsequent care is rooted in the idea that the state owns our lives. They don't. And it's time for critical thinking Americans to take back the freedoms that have been hijacked from us by power hungry politicians. This country was built on self-reliance, not socialism. We the people are responsible for our own bodies and our own lives, and it's time we start demanding that these invasive laws be repealed. It's really not about the seat belt or helmet, but the core philosophy that created the law. If we continue to acquiesce and allow our freedoms to be systematically eliminated, the land of the free will become the land of the incarcerated. The United States already has seven million people in prison, the most of any country in the world. The

U.S. prison population has quadrupled since 1980. It's clearly out of control. The more of these ridiculous laws we create, the higher this number will climb. You may not go to jail for failing to wear a helmet or seat belt, but the mindset that created these laws is a virus that could spread to almost anything. It's scary and it needs to stop. Only critical thinking can make that happen.

"There's absolutely no way you can justify the imposition of safety requirements on autos and motorcycles to protect the drivers of those vehicles."

— Milton Friedman, Nobel Prize Winner in Economics

CRITICAL THINKING QUESTION

What will be the next individual freedom the government will attempt to take away from us?

RECOMMENDED RESOURCE

Why Government is the Problem,
by Milton Friedman

HOMELAND SECURITY

The Department of Homeland Security (DHS) was created in response to the 9/11 attacks. It now boasts over 200,000 employees and has multiple agencies. The DHS is as much about political maneuvering as it is about defense and has received an enormous amount of criticism for being ineffective and poorly managed. Massive in size and boasting a 55 billion dollar budget, the scope of protection the DHS is designated to protect is overwhelming, which is probably the reason it's failing. The American public would never have approved of an agency with such massive power if it weren't for the fear generated on September 11, 2001, which is one of the arguments often cited by conspiracy theorists. This is the same theory many people have about the bombing of Pearl Harbor and Oklahoma City. The idea is that in order for the government to rally the American people to wage war or relinquish their civil liberties, you have to frighten them to the point where they believe they have no choice. Maybe President Roosevelt did know about the Japanese. I don't know. But in the age of the Internet and 24-hour-news, a 9/11 government-led conspiracy would have been almost impossible. That being said, the Bush administration wasted no time reacting to the attack by creating laws like the Patriot Act, which gives the government rights they legally shouldn't have. We complied because we were scared. Terrorism is the cause and less liberty is the effect. If the government suspects you to be a terrorist, they can arrest and detain you on suspicion alone, even if you're an American citizen. Proponents of this measure insist it's necessary for public safety; opponents claim it's unconstitutional. While many people believe these kinds of measures are created with the best intentions, others see them as a slippery slope. The critical thinking question is where does the government's authority end and our personal liberties begin? Once the genie is out of the bottle, how do you put it back in? How much more freedom are we willing to relinquish in the name of fear? And are we really safer than we were before 9/11? More Americans die from lightning strikes every year than terrorist attacks, so aren't we overreacting to the fear we felt on 9/11? Logical thinking needs to replace the emotional thinking that is attempting to turn America into the largest gated community in the world. I'm all for safety, but like a lot of things in government, this is about control and power. Politicians are power hungry, and the more bureaucracy they create the more power they wield. If Washington had its way, we would all be waking up to Uncle Sam's orders and living our lives according to their standards and guidelines. The

DHS has been handed an impossible task and it needs to be broken down, reevaluated, and restructured. And we need the private sector to do it. You can't have government departments evaluating themselves and expect objectivity. That's delusional thinking. If we don't get control of the DHS soon, it will continue to expand; unchecked and unchallenged. Critical thinking says it's time for citizens to stand up and demand accountability, and the first step is engaging an objective third party evaluation to assess the department top to bottom, from its strategies to its scope of work. I promise you the private sector will scrutinize the DHS practices much more severely than any government authority.

"The DHS is as much about political maneuvering as it is defense and has received an enormous amount of criticism for being ineffective and poorly managed. Massive in size and boasting a 55 billion dollar budget, the scope of protection the DHS is designated to protect is overwhelming, which is probably the reason it's failing."

CRITICAL THINKING QUESTION

Wouldn't the private sector do a better job at protecting us than the government?

RECOMMENDED RESOURCE

Homeland Security, by Larry Gaines and Victor Kappeler

TERRORISM

Terrorism is in the eye of the beholder. One man's terrorist is another's freedom fighter, it simply depends on which side of the street you're standing. Terrorism has been around for a long time, and if history serves as a guide, it will be around forever. Terrorism is about coercion through force; physical, psychological or emotional. It's bullying on a grand scale. The delusion is that modern day terrorism against America is about foreigners envying our freedom and high standard of living. The vast majority of terrorism is driven by religion, and the fastest growing groups of terrorists are religious extremists. The 9/11 hijackers were highly educated people with grand delusions of virgins and martyrdom. They killed 3,000 innocent Americans whose only crime was being at work. Were these hijackers born killers, or born-again killers? This is the elephant in the room the leaders of this country are pretending doesn't exist. According to the Department of Homeland Security, the fastest growing sector of terrorist groups are religious in character or motivation. Larry Gaines and Victor Kappeler state in their book, Homeland Security, that "Terrorism predicated on religion often leads to more violence as compared to terrorism that emerges for secular reasons." This shouldn't surprise any first year critical thinker. Religious zealotry is a license to interpret scripture any way one sees fit with the delusion of being personally directed by God himself. After all, they reason, if God wants me to slaughter 3,000 innocent people, who am I to say no? This is not to downplay secular terrorism, but to deny that religious zealotry is the most serious threat to the survival of the world is irrational. It's a mindset fueled by the passion of emotional delusion. The scariest part of this equation is that America is home to millions of religious zealots who believe God talks to them. Who knows what God is whispering in their ears? International terrorism is not the only problem. Domestic terrorism is just as frightening. Bombing an abortion clinic is no different than blowing up an army base. Terrorism is terrorism. A 15-year-old high school girl recently challenged her school's right to display a religious banner in the school's gymnasium and won. Now she's receiving death threats from Christians in her community, and last week her state congressman was interviewed and called the girl "evil." Is this not psychological terrorism rooted in evangelical ignorance? This congressman should be ashamed of himself. He's probably an otherwise intelligent person, but that's the problem with religious zealotry: it drowns people in emotion and makes them stupid. One day it's bullying a 15–year-old girl, and the next it's killing innocent people in the name of God. It's only one non-linear emotional leap away. Critical thinking says we need to get control of our own religious extremists before we judge others. We need to elect serious leaders who make decisions out of critical thinking instead of wishful thinking. This is not an indictment of religion. Everyone in America is free to believe anything they wish. But in the age of suitcase-sized bombs that can blow up a city block, we can no longer afford to whistle past the graveyard. The world's survival is at stake, and if America is truly the leader of the free world, we should prove it by keeping religion and religious zealots out of Washington. American politicians rank among the biggest hypocrites I've ever encountered when it comes to proclaiming their religious faith. Have we had enough sex scandals in Washington to prove my point, or should I list them? Politicians know they must proclaim their Christian faith in order to get elected. This is a joke among political operatives. Confessing faith in a book written by God shouldn't be criteria for a candidate. It belongs in the church and the home, not in Washington. If we don't evolve in this area soon, there won't be an America. And without America, the world as we know it is over. Critical thinking demands that we grow up emotionally and save our wishful thinking for Sunday. On Monday, we operate from objective reality. We can create all the agencies we want to fight terrorism and spend trillions of dollars doing it, but until we remove the motivation for terrorism our efforts will be futile.

"That's the problem with religious zealotry: it

drowns people in emotion and makes them stupid.

One day it's bullying a 15-year-old girl, and the

next its killing innocent people in the name of God.

It's only one non-linear emotional leap away."

CRITICAL THINKING QUESTION

Will America stand up to the religious
zealotry that fuels terrorism quickly
enough to prevent a nuclear event
that will end the world?

RECOMMENDED RESOURCE

The History of Terrorism: From
Antiquity to al Qæda, by Gérard
Chaliand and Arnaud Blin

DEATH PENALTY

The death penalty is one of the most hotly debated topics of our time. In a 2011 Gallup poll, 65% of Americans were in favor of this ultimate punishment. This is down from a 1994 poll, which found that 80% of Americans were pro death penalty. Opponents make the point that the arbitrariness of the death penalty, and the potential of putting an innocent person to death are sufficient reasons for abolishment. Proponents claim we have no proof of ever putting an innocent person to death, while admitting that it's possible. They say the death penalty is a deterrent to murderers and other criminals considering committing a capital offense. Supreme Court Justice Antonin Scalia says, "You want a fair death penalty? You kill, you die. That's fair." When another Supreme Court Justice, John Paul Stevens, was asked if an innocent person had ever been executed in America, he said, "I don't know, but it's certainly possible." Other legal experts claim that receiving the death penalty or life in prison ultimately comes down to money, and the defense you can afford. Reverend Jesse Jackson, an outspoken opponent, claims that people like O.J. Simpson have been set free because he had the means to hire superior counsel. In other words, capital punishment means those without capital get punished. Money plays an additional role in that it costs up to three times as much to impose the death penalty as it does to incarcerate an inmate for life. Convicts can spend decades on death row, all the while appealing their conviction. One of the biggest questions involves the efficacy of the death penalty. In other words, does it work to deter crime? "We don't know if the death penalty deters crime at all. We think it does, but we don't know for sure," says Stephen Markman, former assistant attorney general in the Reagan Administration. Markman also refutes the idea that it's an issue of race, since blacks represent only 12% of the American population and 55% of the prison population. According to Markman, 38% of all murders in America are committed by whites and 47% are committed by blacks, yet 56% of those who are executed are whites and only 38% are blacks. 16/1000 whites receive the death penalty while only 12/1000 blacks receive it. These statistics seem to destroy the race argument, but many people still believe blacks and poor people are most likely to die in the electric chair. This debate will go on, but the delusional thinking in the death penalty equation is based on the logic of deterring vicious criminals from killing people. As I've stated, proponents would love to make this claim but they can't. There are simply too many variables involved to support it. Critical thinking tells us that the extermination of a convicted murderer is about emotional and psychological revenge for the victim's family, and for society as a whole. It plays to our innate human desire for fair play. Not too many people shed tears when they hear of a killer being executed. To the contrary, we feel good for the victim's family that they can now gain closure and move on with their lives. It's the same emotional thinking that drives us to cheer the homeowner who kills a burglar that threatened his family. It makes me feel good, too. So why is it that we can smile at the violent death of another human being? Our sense of fair play. It's pervasive across the animal kingdom, and human beings are no exception. How many of us were saddened to see Osama bin Laden get shot in the head? No one, because he killed 3,000 people. The death penalty appeals to our deepest emotions and works to satisfy our need to even the score and balance the scale.

"You want a fair death penalty? You kill, you die. That's

fair." — Supreme Court Justice Antonin Scalia

CRITICAL THINKING QUESTION

*If someone you loved was murdered, would
your desire to have the killer executed
be rooted more in justice or revenge?*

RECOMMENDED RESOURCE

*Peculiar Institution: America's Death Penalty
in an Age of Abolition,* by David Garland

THE PATIENT PROTECTION AND AFFORDABLE CARE ACT (OBAMACARE)

President Obama and his Democratic colleagues succeeded in ramming through the most massive healthcare legislation in American history without a single Republican vote, and against the will of the American people. The bill was drafted and rushed through so fast that even the people who voted on it didn't have time to read it. Then Speaker of the House Nancy Pelosi, said: "We have to pass this bill so you can find out what's in it," a statement so irresponsible you would expect to hear it in a skit on Saturday Night Live. But this is no joke, and Obamacare is a serious threat to our economy, national security, and way of life. America is 15 trillion dollars in debt and climbing, with no strategy in place to reduce it. America doesn't have to be destroyed by a foreign enemy because we are fully capable of self-destruction. The greatest threat we face is a national debt that weakens our ability to borrow more money when we need it. In his book, The Obamacare Disaster, Peter Ferrara details some of the biggest problems with this law, including higher taxes, lower quality care, runaway government spending, and higher deficits. The young voters who helped put Obama in office are going to be paying for that decision for the rest of their lives. The debt is quickly reaching the point of no return, where we have no way to pay off the principal while the interest accrues. The Democrats forced Obamacare through because no fiscal conservative would endorse it. They made sure there was no time for anyone to study it, and it worked. The delusional thinking is that passing Obamacare was about protecting the 32 million uninsured Americans. It was not. Why would you saddle 300 million people with a mountain of debt they have no way to repay if all you needed was to find a way to cover 10% of the population? Critical thinking tells us that this was an act designed to gain power over people by creating another massive entitlement program that fosters physical and emotional dependency on the government. Think about it: we are now required by law to purchase a product, and if we don't, Big Brother will fine us. Obamacare will require the creation of over 150 new bureaucracies, agencies, boards, and commissions to oversee and operate it. This is a power grab of the highest order, and we allowed it to happen. The potential negative implications are staggering, including bankruptcy. "In health care, as in any other economic arrangement, control of money is power. The question remaining is then: who gets the power, the government or the patient? Patient power will always serve the needs of the people far better than bureaucrats managing the decline of a government-run system on the verge of bankruptcy," says Congressman Paul Ryan. The Democrats seem hell-bent on creating a socialized state while the Republicans are attempting to legislate morality. The only party that operates using critical thinking seems to be the Libertarian party, and they have no interest in controlling our money or our personal lives. If the Founding Fathers were alive today, I believe many would be Libertarians. The parties in power want as much control of our lives as we'll allow them to take; and if Obamacare is not repealed the liberties we will forfeit over time will extend far beyond healthcare. The critical thinking question we have to ask ourselves as Americans is: How much more of our money are we going to permit them to spend and how many more of our freedoms will we allow them to take? It's our country, and we don't answer to Washington. Washington answers to us. The last remaining mystery is, when we decide to take our country back from the bureaucrats, will there still be a country to take back?

"Speaker of the House Nancy Pelosi, said:, 'We have to pass this bill so you can find out what's in it,' a statement so irresponsible you would expect to hear it in a skit on Saturday Night Live."

CRITICAL THINKING QUESTION

Shouldn't lawmakers be required by law to read and understand a bill before they vote it into law?

RECOMMENDED RESOURCE

Why Obamacare is Wrong for America, by Grace-Marie Turner, James Capretta, Thomas Miller and Robert Moffit

FEDERAL DEFICIT

As of May, 2012, the federal debt of the United States Government is approximately $15,488,296,248,000. We are paying approximately 250 billion dollars a year in interest. The U.S. is the world's largest economy, which is around 14 trillion dollars per year. Most economists say that a healthy economy is a debt to gross domestic product (GDP) ratio of 30-70%. In 2007, we reached the 70% mark and in the five years since, we are now over 100%. The most frightening aspect of this issue is we have no strategy in place to pay this money back. The train is off the tracks, and if we don't get it back on soon, we are risking our grandkids future as well as the very survival of America. Compare this with China, the world's second largest economy, which boasts a healthy 43% debt to GDP ratio. Japan, the third largest, is even worse off than us at 180% debt to GDP. The heart of the problem is the U.S. collects about 2.6 trillion dollars per year in income but spends about 4 trillion dollars. You don't have to be an economist to see the problem. The scariest part is that many politicians don't seem overly concerned with this issue, which is clearly the greatest threat to our national security. Forget about the Chinese or Iranians invading America; the real threat is when we declare bankruptcy, and the money well runs dry. Then what do we do? Skyrocketing healthcare costs are a big part of the problem, and Obamacare will only exacerbate it. Since 1970, the United States Government has run a deficit in all but four years. Imagine running your personal finances this way. We would all be in jail. The only reason the Government can get away with it is the unlimited, unregulated power of the Federal Reserve. When the Government runs out of money, the Fed prints more. This is obviously unsustainable, and we are quickly reaching the point of no return. The delusional thinking on the deficit is that it's necessary for America to operate. In other words, Government leaders believe we can't survive unless we fund huge expenses like the Iraq and Afghanistan wars, which cost over 2 trillion dollars of borrowed money plus interest. Think about how ridiculous this expenditure was. Osama bin Laden and his Al Qaida network of terrorists, a well-financed but relatively small sect of terrorists, fly two planes into the World Trade Centers and kill 3,000 Americans. Should we have retaliated? Of course. But to spend 10 years bombing countries that never attacked us is suspect. Meanwhile, it took us 10 years to find and kill bin Laden. Couldn't we have just focused on that instead of launching two wars on two different countries? I don't think Seal Team Six, who killed bin Laden, would have cost two trillion dollars. Now that we are out of Iraq and leaving Afghanistan, the politicians are beating the drums of war with Iran. Here's a critical thinking news flash for Washington: We're broke. Actually, we're beyond broke. We can't afford to invade Iran. Unless they are beating down our borders, or bombing us, we should stop saber rattling and get serious about solving the real threat to our national security—the national debt. The world has changed and so has the way we combat our enemies. In the age of technology, there are smarter ways of keeping America safe. The emotionally charged thinking of political leaders has put us in an economic hole that's going to be difficult to climb out of. The problem is it's sexier to bomb an enemy than to reduce a bloated bureaucracy. What we need is more critical thinking in Washington, and that starts with eliminating the debt, reducing the size of government, and getting our fiscal house in order before it's too late.

"Here's a critical thinking news flash for Washington: We're broke. Actually, we're beyond broke. We can't afford to invade Iran. Unless they are beating down our borders, or bombing us, we should stop saber rattling and get serious about solving the real threat to our national security—the national debt."

CRITICAL THINKING QUESTION

Wouldn't it be wise to legalize all the victimless crimes that are flooding our jails and pay off the national debt with tax revenues and savings from drugs, prostitution, and gambling?

RECOMMENDED RESOURCE

America's Ticking Bankruptcy Bomb: How the Looming Debt Crisis Threatens The American Dream—And How We Can Turn The Tide Before It's Too Late, by Peter Ferrara

PATRIOT ACT

The Patriot Act was constructed to give the department of justice more power to investigate terrorism and was passed into law on October 26, 2001. Since then it's become one of the most controversial laws in American history. Part of the problem is the haste with which it was shoved through Congress in the midst of 9/11 and the anthrax attacks. Then attorney general John Ashcroft took advantage of Congress and a public that was in shell shock and too frightened to challenge it. The Patriot Act is so sweeping it would have been virtually impossible to pass it at any other time. It violates multiple amendments, invades our privacy, and tramples on our civil liberties. It's a slam dunk to be repealed, but here's the problem: it's working. Experts claim it's been responsible for thwarting at least 45 terrorist attacks on American soil. I sleep better at night knowing that my government is using state of the art technology to protect us from radical extremists. I realize this might sound naïve, and maybe it is. I recognize Ashcroft's power grab and the manipulative way in which this legislation was passed. I'm a Libertarian-leaning social liberal who cherishes personal freedom. But the fact is we're thwarting attacks while preserving the American way of life. I realize that some of our personal liberties have been invaded, but none of us is walking down the street fearing a terror attack as the terrorists promised we would. Outside of being semi-molested by the TSA screeners at the airport, we have gone back to our pre 9/11 way of life. And I don't know about you, but after 9/11 I wondered if America would ever be the same. I think it is, and as much as I hate to admit it, I attribute some of our success to the Patriot Act. The delusional thinking is that we can afford to completely repeal it and be just as safe. We can't. The world is a more dangerous place than it's ever been, and an upgrade of our domestic defense system was long overdue. We lived in a protective bubble for so long that most Americans (including me) felt like we were immune to terrorism. We were wrong, and thousands of innocent citizens died as a result of our naiveté. Critical thinking says we need some modified form of the Patriot Act, but this law clearly needs to undergo extensive reform and additional congressional oversight. The idea that the FBI can bug your house, seize your property, and not inform you for months is ludicrous. The part of the act that says possession of a controlled substance is considered an act of terrorism is ridiculous. The government being empowered to legally jail U.S. citizens for an extended amount of time without trial is clearly an abuse of power. There are so many other questionable sections of this law, it would require the remainder of this book to cover them all. Ashcroft and his cronies clearly took advantage of an emotionally wounded Congress and public, and reform is absolutely necessary. Judge Andrew Napolitano, an outspoken opponent, said this: "The Patriot Act is the most abominable, unconstitutional, hateful piece of legislation since the Alien and Sedition Acts." Criticism from the founders comes from beyond the grave when they warned us: "Don't be willing to give up liberty for security." Of course that was long before the days of bombs that fit into briefcases.The government's main role is to protect us and they need 21st century technology to succeed. With some thoughtful modifications and rigorous oversight, the Patriot Act could become truly patriotic.

"The Patriot Act is so sweeping it would have been virtually impossible to pass it at any other time. It's violates multiple amendments, invades our privacy as citizens, and tramples on our civil liberties. It's a slam dunk to be repealed, but here's the problem: it's working."

CRITICAL THINKING QUESTION

If the Patriot Act hadn't passed, would we have experienced another 9/11?

RECOMMENDED RESOURCE

Patriot Acts: What Americans Must Do to Save the Republic, by Catherine Crier

RELIGION

RELIGION IN AMERICA

According to a 2011 Gallup Poll, 92% of Americans believe in a God they've never seen and cannot prove. Christianity is forced on us in childhood, and we are threatened to choose between conformity and damnation. We are warned to worship Jesus or burn in hell. Organized religion has controlled the masses in America for over 200 years. The decision to accept Jesus as lord and savior is not usually made through logic, but from the emotional bullying of a puritanical society. Most Americans don't reach their religious conclusions through research. In fact, very few Americans possess much knowledge on Christianity beyond what their pastor tells them on Sunday. Studies show that fewer than 10% of professed Christians have actually read the entire Bible, and only a fraction of those have seriously studied it. Only a tiny percentage of the faithful have made a conscious decision to be Christians based on in-depth study of it. They believe because they are brainwashed to believe. And God help anyone who doesn't, because Christians can be vicious when their beliefs are even lightly challenged. This malice is rooted in fear, personal insecurities, and lack of proof in their beliefs. The most frightening part of organized religion in America is that so many people refuse to discuss it intelligently and unemotionally. When it comes to religion, many people operate with the emotional maturity of a child. Americans are so terrified of their mortality that they willingly suspend their critical thinking and believe almost anything that eases their fear and offers them comfort. Science is seen as a threat and is often not welcome in the religious debate. Scientists, agnostics, and atheists are savagely attacked for having the audacity to question the beliefs of people living their lives through blind faith.

On the other side of the spectrum you have staunch atheists who are usually more educated on religion than most religious people. Estimates of the size of this group range from 5-15% of the population, but is likely much larger because so many are afraid to speak out.

The delusion of religion is not whether or not God exists, but in the absolute certainty of knowing the unknowable. The staunch atheist who claims to know God does not exist is as guilty as the far right fundamentalist. Both claim to possess information they don't have. Does God exist? No one knows, yet billions of otherwise intelligent people claim to know something they cannot prove.

You might be wondering why I am willing to express my

views knowing I will be ferociously attacked. The answer is simple: America is the last hope in this world. If we can't grow up emotionally and engage in a critical thinking debate, what hope is there for the rest of the world? In the age of briefcase-sized bombs that can blow up a city block, religious extremists are getting more dangerous every day. America is the only country powerful enough to stop them. If we don't, they will destroy the world. Maybe in our lifetime. Not because they are stupid or uneducated. They are not. These are smart people living in a fantasy world where God tells them to destroy the infidel. If the U.S.—the only country strong enough to stop them—is living a similar fantasy, who will save the world? Isn't it time we started thinking for ourselves? Isn't it time to we started taking responsibility for our own lives and stopped relying on a supernatural savior? The savior is America—and the time is now.

EVOLUTION

Charles Darwin shocked the world in 1859 with his ground breaking book, *The Origin of Species*. Since then, Darwin has become one of the most respected and most hated scientists in history. People seeking answers to the mysteries of life finally had evidence-based science to guide them, and those unwilling to abandon ancient superstitions found their new enemy. And that's been the story of Charles Darwin's Theory of Evolution since 1859. Today, scientists around the world have overwhelming evidence that prove the theory is fact, and many Americans are none too happy about it. According to Gallup, 95% of scientists believe in evolution. An even more staggering statistic is only 16% of American's believe in an evolution that is unguided by God. Dr. Jerry Coyne, considered by many scientists to be the world's foremost expert in evolutionary science, says this about people who disbelieve evolution: "You are perverse, a moron, or you are so blinded by religious considerations that you reject all evidence if you do not see that evolution is true." When asked why people don't believe in something with so much evidence behind it, Dr. Coyne said: "Humans like to think of themselves as special, which is supported by religion. Evolution tells us this is not true, and people don't like that. People also don't like evolution because it turns us into beasts, and therefore they think we will behave like beasts. They believe it takes away our basis for morality, and people don't like that, either." As a non-scientist I agree with Dr. Coyne, but let's face it, the evolution vs. creationism debate has an even bigger motivator: the promise of eternal life. Not a bad product to be selling. Who wouldn't want to believe you're going to live forever in a mansion in the sky, as opposed to darkness after death? Who doesn't want to be reunited with loved ones in the afterlife? Religion markets a more attractive product, and that's the reason it sells. So the scientists have a mountain of irrefutable evidence supporting evolution, and the creationists have a 2,000 year old book. Is this really an intelligent debate, or an exercise in wishful thinking? Are most Americans really looking at the facts or simply following the religious dogma they've been brainwashed with since childhood? The delusion is that evolution is still a theory, which according to scientists, it's not. It's a fact, and it's time for Americans to stop pretending the evidence doesn't exist. Believe me, if there was serious evidence of a supernatural creator, I'd be thrilled. I miss my late friends and family and would love to see them again. The problem is there's no evidence to support such a being. We all have the choice of operating from emotion-based faith without evidence or logic-based science with lots of it. When it comes to evolution vs. creationism, Americans almost always choose to ignore science and operate from blind faith. To exacerbate the issue, many Americans wear this disbelief in science as a badge of honor, exhibiting arrogance for their ignorance. Can you imagine if we did this in other areas of life? What if we choose not to believe in the laws of gravity? How about atomic theory? How about the Theory of Relativity? We laugh at the notion of ignoring these scientific theories, yet when it comes to religion, we stick our heads in the sand and believe in tales of a talking snake, burning bush, and a boat with every species of animal on it. And to think some people see America as a socially progressive country!

Not accepting evolution as a fact is engaging in the willful suspension of critical thinking. Wishful thinking is nice for children, but when you're the most powerful country on the planet it's a little embarrassing. We need to teach our kids the facts about evolution and present the evidence with the same fervor as the preacher delivers his Sunday sermon, and then challenge them to think for themselves. How many of us can actually explain the theory of evolution in a coherent manner? My guess is very few, because in some circles it's considered blasphemy to even discuss it. It's time we educated ourselves and learned to separate facts from fiction. Once a person is educated enough to explain the basic tenets of both evolution and creationism, he or she is capable of making an intelligent, emotion-free decision based on the evidence. Unfortunately, this is not going to happen anytime soon. The product of eternal life is simply too alluring to call into question, even if it appears to be a fabricated fantasy designed to control society. America is marginalized by socially progressive countries around the world due to this lack of critical thinking, and will never be taken seriously by more sophisticated societies until we overcome our addiction to superstition. George W. Bush proclaimed on national television that God wanted all people around the world to be free. I guess he missed the part in the Bible that endorses slavery and subjugation of women. You'd expect this statement from an uneducated third world leader, but from the leader of the free world?

The United States ranks 33rd in the world when it comes to our citizens' belief in evolution. Only the country of Turkey is ranked lower. "American Protestantism is more fundamentalist than anybody except perhaps the Islamic fundamentalist, which is why Turkey and we are so close," said study co-author Jon Miller of Michigan State University. Politics is also contributing to America's widespread confusion about evolution, researchers say. Major political parties in the United States are more willing to make opposition to evolution a prominent part of their campaigns to garner conservative votes—something that does not happen in Europe or Japan. The evolution vs. creationism debate won't end in our lifetime, but hopefully enough people will engage in critical thinking long enough to educate themselves on the evidence and stop believing everything they read in the Bible and hear in church. Education and science are the only things that will eventually solve this debate.

"You are perverse, a moron, or you are so blinded by religious considerations that you reject all evidence if you do not see that evolution is true." — Dr. Jerry Coyne, Evolutionary Scientist, University of Chicago

CRITICAL THINKING QUESTION

Is the lack of belief in evolution among Americans due to ignorance or denial?

RECOMMENDED RESOURCE

Why Evolution is True, by Jerry A. Coyne

CATHOLIC CHURCH

I grew up Lutheran in the northwest suburbs of Chicago in the 1960s and '70s, but almost all of my friends were Catholic and attended Catholic school. They would tell stories about how mean the nuns were and we would laugh. My friends were terrified to disobey the penguins, but I think they developed a healthy respect for their leadership. They treated the priests like gods, which I also found a little strange. The churches in our town were the epicenter of our social network. They helped a lot of people and were good for the community. I rebelled against the coercive dogma I heard being preached on Sundays, but I always respected the institution. If there was sexual abuse happening across the street at the Catholic Church, I never heard about it.

As we've learned in recent years, the depth and breadth of abuse in the Catholic Church around the world is almost unbelievable. The revelations of the past 10 years have effectively wiped out the good deeds of the Catholic Church and demolished its credibility. The sad fact is, the Catholic Church has been guilty of sexual impropriety among its clergy for 2,000 years, and all the leadership, right up to the Papacy, has known about it. In *Sex, Priests, and Secret Codes: The Catholic Church's 2,000 Year Paper Trail of Sexual Abuse*, an outstanding book published in 2006, the authors say: "Unfortunately, this crime—and that is its proper name—has been an open wound on the Body of Christ for as far back as records are kept. History shows that in practically every century since the church began, the problem of clerical abuse of minors was not just lurking in the shadows but so open at times that extraordinary means had to be taken to quell it. If there is anything new about the sexual abuse of minors among members of the clergy, it is that over the past fifty years a conspiracy of silence has covered it."

The Associated Press estimates the cost of the sexual abuse scandal to the church has been well over 3 billion dollars, and those are just the costs we know about. How many billions of dollars have been secretly paid out to victims and covered up by the church? No one knows for sure, but we do know the church leaders were far more interested in protecting their child molesting priests than they than were in the children who trusted them. If you want to see why the church finally woke up and started treating this problem seriously, all you have to do is follow the money trail. In the Catholic Church, money talks. Father Thomas P. Doyle, who served at the Vatican Embassy, said this: "It's one thing to neglect to protect the faithful from sexual predators; it's quite another thing altogether to neglect to protect the church's assets from lawsuits. Action to protect church assets has never faltered or been neglected." After this hurricane of abuse was discovered, and church leaders were confronted with new victims every day, you'd think they would hang their heads in shame. After all, wouldn't this be befitting to the earthly representatives of Christ? You'd think so, but Catholic leaders aren't used to having their authority questioned. The worst example of this is when Pope Benedict XVI, the current Pope, formerly known as Joseph Ratzinger, was discovered to have covered up sexual abuses by a priest in Germany, his defense was: "I will not be intimidated," and he advised a billion Catholics around the world to "Ignore petty gossip." Some people called for his arrest, but the power of the church is unparalleled in both politics and money, and Pope Benedict escaped unscathed by the scandal. The man the church calls the "Vicar of Christ on Earth" is forever linked to the sexual abuse of little boys. Christopher Hitchens, the late author of *God is Not Great*, predicted the Pope would continue to distance himself from the scandal because further inquiry by the Vatican would implicate him. It's a sad state of affairs, but the Pope is not the only high level representative to aid in the cover up. Cardinal Bernard Law, the longtime Roman Catholic archbishop of Boston who was once considered a candidate for Pope, was forced to resign in disgrace when the *Boston Globe*'s investigation uncovered a mountain of Church documents that proved high-ranking officials had repeatedly put the welfare of their priests ahead of that of the children. Many Catholics called for Law's resignation and refused to make further donations to the Church, and that's when Church leadership started to get concerned. Law finally resigned on December 13, 2002, and was assigned to an archpriest position in Rome. He is currently Archbishop Emeritus of Boston. So while Law enjoys Archbishop Emeritus status in the twilight of his life, thousands of children he exposed to child molesting priests struggle to cope. Some have committed suicide. It's like a horror movie where evil wins. It's sad, pathetic, and criminal. But how dare we question or criticize the Catholic Church, the direct representatives of God. After all, they've been getting away with this for 2,000 years. Who are we to stop them now?

There is so much delusional thinking on this subject I don't know which to pick, but let's start with the faith itself. There are 77 million Catholics in the United States and over 1 billion in the world, so here's my critical thinking question:

Has anyone thought to ask where the Catholic God they worship was when these little boys were being anally raped by priests, or was it the devil that made them do it? What kind of a God would allow a 4-year-old child to be raped, bullied and tortured by his representatives on Earth? And this is a loving God?

It's like a school principal who stands by and watches his teachers rape their students and does nothing to stop it...for 2,000 years! So what does the principal eventually do? He moves them to another school so they can rape more little kids. If this happened we would lock the principal up for life. But since its God, we fall to our knees and praise him instead. If it was the 1st century, you might somehow justify that level of ignorance. But this is 2012. Isn't it time we start applying critical thinking to this corrupt religious cult? In one of the most educated countries in the world, are we so frightened of what we will find out about God, religion, and the church that we cannot bring ourselves to challenge these entities? Are we so afraid to die that that we consciously choose wishful thinking over critical thinking? Our failure as a society to subject the Catholic Church to the scrutiny of critical inquiry is shameful. It's time for us to grow up and start facing facts about ancient superstition and religious mythology. How much more abuse and manipulation has to occur before we wake up and realize we are the only ones who can stop it. And if God does exist, he apparently can't be bothered to intervene when his disciples are anally raping little children. When will Americans wake up to objective reality and see the world the way it is instead of the way we wish it was.

"And if God does exist, he apparently can't be bothered to intervene when his disciples are anally raping little children"

CRITICAL THINKING QUESTION

How many more children will be raped and abused by priests before we begin executing these child molesters?

RECOMMENDED RESOURCE

Sex, Priests, and Secret Codes: The Catholic Church's 2,000 Year Paper Trail of Sexual Abuse by Thomas P. Doyle, A.W. Richard Sipe and Patrick J. Wall

SCHOOL PRAYER

School prayer is always a hotly debated issue. Constitutionalists claim that any religious ritual performed as part of public school curriculum violates the First Amendment's establishment clause. Fundamentalist Christians are convinced that ending faculty-led school prayer is equivalent to slapping God in the face. Others see it as the moral downward spiral of America. The United States is the most religiously diverse nation in the world, boasting more than 1,500 religious bodies and sects. There are nearly 360,000 churches, mosques, temples, and synagogues representing millions of members and an untold number of beliefs and philosophies. The idea of a generic school prayer pleasing them all is ridiculous. America is a melting pot with room for all religions and belief systems, but not under one roof. Every public school student is allowed to pray privately, so the statement that we have banned prayer in schools is patently false. We have not banned school prayer. We have banned faculty-led prayer that is organized and sanctioned by the schools. Fundamentalist Christians have damaged their credibility over the past 50 years by proclaiming that the government has "kicked God out of the schools." The faithful are as free to pray as they have always been without making a public display out of a private, personal process. The majority of politicians have supported these protests due to their overwhelming popularity among their constituency. Simply put: if you go against organized religion in America, you're going to have a heck of a time getting elected. Americans are brainwashed from birth to believe, fear, and worship a god that will damn them to hell for eternity or be their best friend, depending on how they conform to the Bible. Of course the interpretation of ancient scripture has thousands of subjective variations, which makes adhering to them and saving your soul tricky business. Before the 1962 Supreme Court decision to ban faculty-led school prayer, (Engel vs. Vitale) the brainwashing began in kindergarten and continued through high school. Since children have no frame of reference to pull from and are highly impressionable, they simply believe everything they hear and repeat the words, phrases and prayers we tell them to repeat. It's the antithesis of independent thought and education, and that's why religious leaders are desperate to have this ruling revoked. The only way to control the masses is to program them as children and motivate them through fear. If you can't control them by the time they're teenagers, they'll begin thinking for themselves and reject fear-based doctrine. If they're not terrified of going to hell by high school, you might as well move on to younger kids. Convincing an intelligent, informed high school sophomore born in the information age of a man living inside a whale, a virgin birth, and a dead man coming back to life is going to be next to impossible—unless you've been brainwashing him from infancy. And that's the real reason the religious have been fighting the Engel vs. Vitale decision for the last 50 years. Simply put, they can't afford not to. They're selling the promise of eternal life, which admittedly is a great product with mass appeal. Their problem is they have no evidence to prove their promise. Their guarantee is that their book was divinely inspired, but once again they lack evidence to back their claim. If they made these claims on an infomercial, the FCC would throw them in jail. But since we're talking about religion, televangelists can sell prayer cloths with supernatural powers, and the FCC allows them all the air time money can buy. School prayer is part of organized religion's overall marketing strategy which commands Christians to believe the Bible with blind faith in exchange for life after death. The upside of eternal life combined with the downside of rotting in hell is enough for most people to suspend their critical thinking. Millions of religiously indifferent Americans believe in school prayer because they feel their kids will benefit from religious indoctrination. They don't believe in superstition, but they think the moral tenets of religion are good. The delusional thinking on school prayer is that it's about a student's spiritual growth and moral development. It's not. School prayer is about controlling the minds of children through systematic programming before they have the desire to think for themselves. They know if they can control them when they're kids they have a good chance of controlling them as adults. Think about it objectively: why would the daily recital of a generic prayer aid the development of a child? It doesn't. I started school in 1970, and every day for the next 13 years we put our hand on our hearts and robotically repeated the Pledge of Allegiance, which by that time had been modified to include the words "under God", which was added in 1954. What good did that drone-like process do? None at all. By the time my friends and I were forced into attending religious studies (CCD and Lutheran Confirmation Classes) we were 12 years old and capable of free thought and some level of critical inquiry. My church pastor and his assistant were pillars in the community whom I respected very much. The content of the classes, however, struck me as more of a series of fairy tales than facts. When I mentioned this in front of the confirmation class and the pastors, I was politely ignored and labeled a troublemaker. The next three years of study only confirmed my original analysis. The lesson I walked away with after 36 months of intense religious studies was that education was the enemy of organized religion. The more you learned, the less you believed, and the less you believed, the less vulnerable you were to the fear-mongering of the church and the bullying of the Bible. If Engel vs. Vitale had been gone the other way, I don't know if I would have ever become an independent critical thinker. It scares me just thinking about it.

"School prayer is about controlling the minds of children through systematic programming before they have the desire to think for themselves."

CRITICAL THINKING QUESTION

Why isn't private prayer in schools good enough for the religious right?

RECOMMENDED RESOURCE

The Battle Over School Prayer: How Engel v. Vitale Changed America, by Bruce J. Dierenfield

MONEY

The Bible has hundreds of references to money, warning the faithful of the dangers of riches and downside of wealth. The most well-known of these references is found in Timothy 6:9-11:

"But those who want to get rich fall into temptation and a snare and many foolish and harmful desires which plunge men into ruin and destruction. For the love of money is a root of all sorts of evil, and some by longing for it have wandered away from the faith and pierced themselves with many griefs. But flee from these things, you man of God, and pursue righteousness, godliness, faith, love, perseverance and gentleness." While no one would recommend falling in love with money, this passage has been used by religious leaders to provide guilt to the ambitious and stifle the successful. In short, it gives the desire for money a bad name, and the people who dream of riches a guilty conscience. Anyone who ever acquired wealth began by envisioning their success. The desire to get rich has driven Americans to become the most innovative, creative population on the planet. Without the incentive of financial prosperity, the steel industry, railroad, intercontinental highway system, and all the technology-driven products developed in America wouldn't have ever been created. Money makes bad people worse and good people better, and most people are good. The Bible is the primary catalyst of negative beliefs about money. And as religious as America is, it's amazing any of the faithful get rich. Many do, but no thanks to the Bible. In Matthew, Jesus said to His disciples, "Truly I say to you, it is hard for a rich man to enter the kingdom of heaven. Again I say to you, it is easier for a camel to go through the eye of a needle, than for a rich man to enter the kingdom of God." Not exactly a motivational speech. It's clear that the authors of the Bible are not fans of overachievers, which is what built America into the economic engine of the world. The idea that's perpetuated throughout the past 2,000 years is that the poor are less materialistic and more spiritual than the rich and therefore closer to God. This is delusional and dangerous, yet many people pride themselves on being poor and shun opportunities to pull themselves up from poverty. The Bible has led them to believe God favors the poor. When you look at the Bible objectively without emotion, it's easy to see that the authors were attempting to control and manipulate the population, and it's far easier to accomplish with the poor than the rich. The most faithful followers of the Bible are the uneducated, poor and downtrodden among us with nowhere else to turn. Hebrews 13:5 hits it again: "Keep your life free from the love of money, and be content with what you have." Imagine if Henry Ford was content with what he had before he changed the world creating mass-production for automobiles? Would anyone say Edison was content? Not to mention hundreds of others who worked tirelessly and changed America. American exceptionalism and contentment with the status quo are mutually incompatible. The masses aren't content because they're always worried about money, and the rich aren't content because they are always striving for more. Anything more than being happily dissatisfied is a recipe for stagnation. People get wealthy through strategic thinking and hard work. When most workers are rushing out the door at five o'clock, the ambitious are still working. The Bible is against this extra effort. Proverbs 23:4 says; "Do not weary yourself to gain wealth, cease from your consideration of it." Not only does God discourage gaining wealth, he doesn't want us to even consider it. Is it any wonder Americans have such negative beliefs about money? We recite these passages in church and Sunday School from the time we can barely read until they bury us in a box. We repeat it so many times for so long that we're convinced it's true. If God is opposed to working yourself weary for success, how can America be God's Country? America is known around the world as the nation of success seekers to the point where we're criticized for our ambition. This is incongruent with what the Bible teaches. It's clear that the authors of the Bible didn't understand what made our financial system work. In Deuteronomy 23:19-20, it says: "You shall not charge interest to your countrymen: interest on money, food, or anything that may be loaned at interest. You may charge interest to a foreigner, but to your countrymen you shall not charge interest, so that the Lord your God may bless you in all that you undertake in the land which you are about to enter to possess." If banks, investors, and financial institutions didn't earn interest on their money, they wouldn't loan it, and if Americans couldn't borrow money, our economy would collapse. How can an all-powerful, omniscient god not know this? America is 15.4 trillion dollars in debt. The interest on that debt is over 20 billion dollars a month. If we lost our ability to borrow, our entire financial system would disintegrate within weeks. As a domino effect of our economic failure, every major economy would also collapse shortly thereafter. This would effectively end the world. There would be martial law, mass rioting and a complete free-for-all in the streets of the world. Hundreds of millions of people would die. In the 21st century, the world is interconnected, and the glue that holds it together is money, trade, lending, and borrowing. Every high school kid knows this, so why doesn't the god that wrote this book? You would expect this level of ignorance from men who lived 2,000 years ago, but if the Bible was inspired by God, how do Christians reconcile these ridiculous statements? The truth is they don't. They simply ignore them. Most of the Christians I interviewed for this book had no idea these passages were even in the Bible. They had been commanded from childhood to take everything they read in this book and everything they heard in church on faith. And these are not stupid people. They've simply been brainwashed to believe the unbelievable and bullied into refusing to exercise independent thought when it comes to the Bible. The saddest part is most of them have been doing this so long they don't even realize it. And if all this isn't bad enough, the passage that bothers me most is found in Philippians 4:19, which says: "And my God will supply all your needs according to His riches in glory in Christ Jesus." If this is true, why are hundreds of millions of people starving around the world? They're not asking for a new Mercedes; they're asking for food. The pain and suffering in the world is unimaginable and has been since before the Bible was written. If God will supply our needs, where has he been for the past 150,000 years? The Bible warns us repeatedly about the love of money, our desire to acquire it, and our chances of entering heaven once we have it, yet He allows the poor to starve in the streets. These people did nothing to deserve this misery, yet the god of the Bible refuses to help. The delusional thinking about the Bible's advice on money is that being powerless and poor is more spiritual than being rich and self-reliant, and that being poor brings you closer to God. The truth is, it's a matter of mass control and manipulation. Poor people are easy to control and manipulate. Rich people are not. And that's why the Bible promotes poverty. Unfortunately, many of the faithful never realize they're being manipulated, and their negative beliefs about money keep them struggling for it their entire lives. These are otherwise intelligent, decent people who are simply so heavily indoctrinated in ancient dogma they are almost assuredly doomed to a life of middle-class mediocrity. Critical thinking says to ignore the Bible's advice on money and seek the counsel of rich people and a well-educated financial advisor.

"The delusional thinking about the Bible's advice on money is that being powerless and poor is more spiritual than being rich and self-reliant, and that being poor brings you closer to god. The truth is it's a matter of mass control and manipulation. Poor people are easy to control and manipulate. Rich people are not."

CRITICAL THINKING QUESTION

Why does the Bible discourage us from aspiring to wealth while the church (collectively) has become one of the richest entities in the world?

RECOMMENDED RESOURCE

God is Not Great: How Religion Poisons Everything, by Christopher Hitchens

THE BIBLE

The Bible is a book of symbolic literature. It's a fusion of stories, ideas, chronologies, and traditions woven together over at least 1,000 years. The authors, editors and the massive organization of people that followed set out to control the world through their view of morality under the threat of eternal damnation for noncompliance, and it worked. This wouldn't be surprising 2,000 or even 200 years ago, but in 2012 it's almost unbelievable. The Bible is promoted as the loving word of God, yet it's filled with murder, hate, intolerance, inhuman slaughter, slavery, torture, homophobia, and discrimination. The Bible is a bully-book. It demands that you follow the authors' barbaric laws of life and living or burn in hell. If you decide to submit to the bully, he rewards with everlasting life. If not, you burn. It's pretty straightforward. It's no different than the bully at school who steals your money and promises you protection, or the mobster who threatens to vandalize your store unless you pay him part of the profits. The Bible is a much bigger bully than both because at least the school bully and street thug don't require that you worship them as they terrorize you. The beasts that wrote the Bible command you to fall to your knees and proclaim your love and devotion to a god that will gladly slaughter you if you don't. It's sick and perverse, but you won't hear much about this on Sunday morning. Religious leaders prefer to focus on the loving side of the Bible God, not the vicious, murderous side. He just reminds you of it once in a while to keep you in line. The delusional thinking is that this book is anything more than an ancient text written, edited, manipulated, and promoted by men who wished to control and manipulate society. There may or not be a God, but the Bible and its terrible tales of sacrificial killings and genocide certainly don't represent Him well. To believe that the Bible is the word of an all knowing personal god requires complete detachment from rational analysis and critical thinking. That being said, it will continue to be popular in a world that's addicted to the emotion of hope. Few people on the planet have the intellectual and emotional capacity to accept their place in the evolutionary chain. It's easier to imagine an all knowing and loving savior coming to the rescue, rewarding them with a mansion in the sky and reuniting them with loved ones. The Bible and its promise of salvation is the greatest story ever sold. It made the Catholic Church the richest, most powerful and corrupt organization in the history of the world. It's led to an endless array of wars, needless killing, and senseless suffering. This is not my opinion, it's history. Yet we continue to close our eyes and pretend the Bible is only full of love, mercy, and hope. It's like bringing a mass murderer home for dinner and introducing him as a kind, caring, man. He may be all those things, but he's also a cold-blooded killer who would just as soon put a knife through your heart as share a meal with your family. I don't think any of us would be willing to worship a psychopath or bring one into our home, but we faithfully fall to our knees and pray to a God that crucified his own kid on a cross and demands that we celebrate his sacrifice. Is this the behavior of an educated people? Critical thinking says people don't believe in the Bible because it's believable; they believe it because they want to believe it. They need to believe it. The prospect of eternal death is too much for most people to bear. So instead of searching for truth, they cling to this book like a drowning man to a life preserver. The most intelligent and emotionally mature people in society know this, yet most allow the delusion to continue in order to avoid panic, depression, and hysteria among the masses. Ignorance is not only bliss, in this case it's the glue that holds civilization together. Brilliant thinkers like Thomas Jefferson, Benjamin Franklin, Albert Einstein, and many other prominent Americans in our history recognized that the Bible wasn't the word of God, yet they purposely tried to appease people by attempting to find the good in a bad book. Thomas Jefferson went as far as writing his own Bible, minus the supernatural stories of talking snakes, burning bushes, and walking on water. In a letter to John

Adams, Jefferson said he had edited out "the nonsense." But even though Jefferson's Bible is over 200 years old, only a tiny percentage Americans have ever heard of it, much less read it. And even if they did, it wouldn't matter. Because without the supernatural promise of salvation, they would have little interest in a book that focuses on the moral teachings of Jesus. Christians love to say that without the Bible, society has no moral code, but the truth is they're far less interested in morality than they are in salvation. The morals outlined in the Bible could be dictated by a 12-year-old. People have one reason and one reason only for having blind faith in a book with no evidence of validity: they can't handle not knowing what happens when they die. The Bible removes their anxiety and calms their fears, no matter how far-fetched the story is. In a time in history when religious zealots are out to destroy America, we need to wake up and start operating from reason and reality and leave superstition behind. When we have senators, congressman, and presidential candidates claiming the answer to the country's problems is prayer, we have a problem. American's won't put their Bibles in the fictional file in our lifetime, but it will happen eventually if the country survives long enough. All superstitions are eventually disproved by science and tucked away as remnants of past ignorance. The Bible will become an ancient relic of the past someday. Until then, we need to have the courage to question and probe every aspect of this book and the multibillion dollar mob that wields it as a weapon. The international crackdown on the extensive abuse of children by the Catholic Church is a start, but that's only the beginning. It's time we start putting polite conversation behind and begin debating the Bible in mixed company. Forget about American Idol and the baseball game. Our very existence is at stake, and many of our policies and politics are driven by what I'm writing about in this book. It's time for Americans to begin engaging in serious discourse regarding the future of this country—before it's too late.

"The beasts that wrote the Bible command you to fall to your knees and proclaim your love and devotion to a God that will gladly slaughter you if you don't."

CRITICAL THINKING QUESTION

Would you even speak to someone that promised you would burn in hell for eternity if you didn't love him?

RECOMMENDED RESOURCE

The God Delusion, by Richard Dawkins

STATE OF THE CHURCH IN AMERICA

The Church is in trouble. While a 2010 Gallup poll based on 800,000 interviews showed that 43.1% of Americans attend church weekly or almost weekly, it's well known among social scientists and church officials that at least 50% of people lie or exaggerate in religiously oriented surveys. Admitting that you're not attending church on a regular basis in America is like saying you don't like baseball or apple pie. It's downright un-American. So Christians, who are taught to exhibit Christ-like behavior, lie. If it weren't for the talking snake tempting Eve in the Garden of Eden, this would never happen. But alas, the numbers are skewed. Let's look at the real statistics:

David T. Olson, from the American Church Research Project, says that the actual percentage of Americans attending church on a weekly or almost basis is closer to 16.9% and declining. 9% are Evangelical, 2.8% are Mainline, and 5.1% are Catholic. While the population in America increased by 62 million people from 1990-2010, the church is not increasing its overall attendance.

According to the Yearbook of American and Canadian Churches, in 1990, 137 million Americans attended church. In 2012 the number increased to 145 million. Churches that have been growing are continuing to grow, and churches that have been in decline are continuing to decline. Growing denominations include the Mormons at 1.6%; The National Baptist Convention, 3.9%; and Assemblies of God, 4%. The rest are in decline. Donations have also decreased by 1.2 billion dollars (2008), but this probably has more to do with the fledging economy and high unemployment than the state of the church. Some Christian leaders claim the primary reason for declining attendance is that Americans are becoming "too self-sufficient." And that statement defines the real issue. The core premise of organized religion is that we are help-less and hopeless without God, and a large percentage of people in their 20s and 30s are rejecting it. These are young adults who never lived in a world without computers, and most of them had access to the Internet as children. They grew up in the instant information age and they know how to find answers faster than any generation in history. As a result, they are smarter and savvier, and the idea that they are hopeless sinners who should fall to their knees and beg forgiveness doesn't make sense to them. It's easy to fool an uneducated populous, especially when you're offering eternal life in exchange for rational thought. But when the populous has access to all of the world's knowledge at their fingertips, it changes the game. This new generation is also aware of the abuses of the church and religious leaders. A 30-year-old man is much more likely to know the details of the Catholic Priest Sex Scandal than a man twice his age. These kids have more access to information on their phones than we did in every library we ever visited and every encyclopedia we ever owned. They are better educated, more sophisticated, and highly skeptical. Telling them they are helpless without Jesus minus the evidence to prove it isn't going to fly. My generation and the generations before me were taught to respect our elders and submit to authority. The new generations are equally respectful but eager to challenge unsubstantiated claims, superstitions, and anything that sounds suspect. It's the upward intellectual evolution of society, and its bad news for the Church. The delusional thinking is that the church's decline is a bad thing. It's not. If people were meeting on Sunday morning to discuss strategies to reduce human suffering, irresponsible behavior that harms others, ending violence in their neighborhoods, and other critical issues, a declining membership would be a tragedy. But convening weekly to learn more about a book filled with hate, bigotry, and murder that promises to save your soul is an exercise in mass delusion and dangerous to society. Sending our kids to interact with celibate Catholic priests is still dangerous. Critical thinking says we should restructure the church by removing the medieval practices and superstitions and focus on uplifting society through lessons of personal responsibility, friendship, and charity. The faster the church stops telling people they are hopeless sinners and starts building them up the better chance this archaic institution has to survive. It's a parallel to the evolutionary theory of natural selection, and time will tell whether church leaders are smart enough to survive.

"Critical thinking says we should restructure the church by removing the medieval practices and superstitions and focus on uplifting society through lessons of personal responsibility, friendship, and charity. The faster the church stops telling people they are hopeless sinners and starts building them up the better chance this archaic institution has to survive"

CRITICAL THINKING QUESTION

With millions of Americans living in poverty, an economy on the verge of collapse and the omnipresence of global terrorism, is sitting in church hearing how we are hopeless, helpless sinners really the best use of our time?

RECOMMENDED RESOURCE

The End of Faith: Religion, Terror and the Future of Reason, By Sam Harris

GOD

I attended a Lutheran Church regularly until I was 17 years old. I studied to be confirmed for three years. I've read dozens of books detailing all the major religions, interviewed hundreds of people on this subject, from the faithful to the new atheists. I've shared the stage with some of the biggest televangelists in the world, and for the past 24 months, I've watched hundreds of hours of video footage from some of the greatest minds in America discussing and debating whether or not God exists. From Christian apologetic Dr. William Lane Craig to evolutionary biologist Richard Dawkins. After investing all of this time and energy searching for an answer to whether or not God exists, here is my conclusion:

I don't know.

I know you were probably hoping for a better answer, but that's the best I have. I don't know if there's a God, but here's the thing: neither do you. And neither does William Lane Craig, Sam Harris, Billy Graham, or Richard Dawkins. And neither does the Pope, who after you remove the robe and skull cap, is just a man. No one knows for sure what happens when you die, and if they tell you they do, hang on to your wallet because the pitch is coming.

I personally hope there is a God. Not the God of the Bible, but a loving, caring creator that would guide us to the next realm, if such a realm exists. That would be really nice.

I hope there's a heaven, too. Not the one in the Bible that's the opposite of hell, but a peaceful place to rest without war, poverty, or human suffering. And no income tax would be a bonus.

My dad died a few months ago, and I miss him. I'd like to see him again; and maybe even hit a few tennis balls together. That would be fun.

As comforting as all this would be, I'm not betting on it. I think it's unlikely. But no one knows for sure, and I'll hope for the best. I'll remain open-minded and welcome credible evidence if it's ever presented.

If there is a God, you won't find Him in the Bible or the church, but inside your own heart. I'd suggest searching there first. A God that allows his people to suffer needlessly is not a God worth worshipping. Instead, we need to look inside ourselves and band together as human beings to end the misery that visits so many. It's time to stop praying to an invisible man in the sky and start taking steps to reduce human suffering. As far as establishing a moral code without the Bible as our guide, that's simply common sense. Treat people the way you want to be treated. Don't hurt anyone, take their stuff, or infringe on their rights. Obey the laws established by society. If you can give someone a hand when they need it, that's always a good thing. You're not obligated to, but throwing in a little charity is always nice. We all need a little help sometimes.

And there's your moral code.

No need to carve it in stone or hand it down from a mountain. Just remember to be fair and nice to yourself and others. Did we ever really need a supernatural being or a book to tell us these things?

I think we'll be just fine on our own.

All we need to do is start thinking for ourselves.

"I personally hope there is a God. Not the God of the Bible, but a loving, caring creator that would guide us to the next realm, if such a realm exists. That would be really nice"

CRITICAL THINKING QUESTION

Is there way we could take the best teachings of all religions, remove the fear, hate, and superstition and create a better country for our grandchildren to inherit?

RECOMMENDED RESOURCE

The Jefferson Bible: The Life and Morals of Jesus of Nazareth, by Thomas Jefferson

LEARNING RESOURCES

- *177 Mental Toughness Secrets*
  www.mentaltoughnesssecrets.com

- *177 Mental Toughness Secrets - CD Album*
  www.mentaltoughnesssecrets.com

- *Coaching 177 Mental Toughness Secrets*
  www.coachingmentaltoughness.com

- *Mental Toughness Blog*
  www.MentalToughnessBlog.com

- *Mental Toughness College*
  www.mentaltoughnesscollege.com

- *Mental Toughness University*
  www.mentaltoughnessuniversity.com

- *Mental Toughness University Licensee*

- *The Making of a Million Dollar Mind*
  www.milliondollarmind.com

- *Mental Toughness Mastery*
  www.mentaltoughnessmastery.com

- *Fatloser - Mental Toughness for Weight Control*
  www.fatloser.com

- *Die Fat or Get Tough*
  www.diefatbook.com

- *How Rich People Think*
  www.howrichpeoplethinkbook.com

- *Steve on TV*
  www.SteveOnTV.com

- *Speaker Steve Siebold*
  www.speakerstevesiebold.com

- *Bill Gove Speech Workshop*
  www.feepaidprofessionalspeaker.com

- *Public Speakers Blog*
  www.publicspeakersblog.com

- *Free Speaking Course*
  www.freespeakingcourse.com

- *Sex Politics Religion Blog*
  www.sexpoliticsreligionblog.com

- *Sex Politics Religion Blog Talk Radio*
  www.blogtalkradio.com/sexpoliticsreligion

- *Siebold Success Network*
  www.ssnlive.org

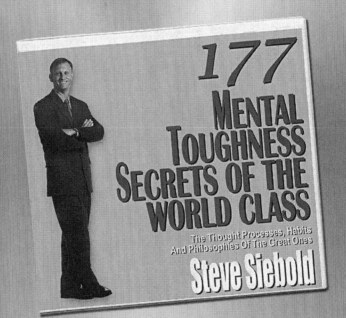

FREE Video Updates on

MENTAL TOUGHNESS

with Steve Siebold

Join The Discussion! Subscribe Today at

www.MentalToughnessBlog.com

Mental Toughness University
Helps Companies Increase Sales And Move
Market Share By Creating A No Excuses-High
Performance Culture

Mental Toughness University is a comprehensive mental training process that moves sales and management teams from good to great. Mental Toughness trains people how to control their thoughts, feelings, and attitudes, before, during and after a performance. Especially under pressure.

What Are The Benefits of Mental Toughness Training?

Most MTU corporate clients are sales and management teams that report dramatic increases in sales. Management teams benefit by learning how to coach the mental toughness process and implement it immediately into their daily coaching with their sales team. Managers often adopt new criteria for hiring salespeople after completing the course. Employee retention rates are also affected due to the personal benefits gained during the training. MTU delivers both professional and personal results. Since most research shows that an employee's job is not the most important aspect of his or her life, the ongoing personal benefits of this program tend to raise the switching cost of an employee moving to another company. Companies often experience enhanced customer service from the participants as a result of their new level of focus on the customer.

Mental Toughness University is Not a Traditional Training Program.
MTU is a Process, Not a Program.

It's about training people how to THINK like world-class performers, and how to control and manipulate their own emotions for MAXIMUM performance. MTU is a cross between emotional intelligence training and critical thinking. It's an introspective process that causes people to examine their thoughts, feelings attitudes, and beliefs and how they are directly impacting their results. We call the process, 'Facilitated Introspection'. The six-hour program is an awakening to expose participants to the process and show them there's a higher level of emotional competence and mental performance than they are experiencing. MTU facilitates this emotional transformation over the next 12 months during the teleconference follow up program. Each participant is assigned 20 minutes of homework each week and held accountable for submitting it. Both the six-hour seminar and the follow-up teleconferences are highly interactive. Most people that go through the process have never been exposed to this level of personal introspection. They may be familiar with some of the content, but the real growth and change comes from them getting to know themselves. Most participants are shocked and surprised to learn how little they know about themselves. The Mental Toughness University Process has the power to bring out the best in any performer who will engage his or her mind in the process.

For more information, visit www.mentaltoughnessuniversity.com

"IMAGINE YOUR CAREER SPEAKING, TRAINING AND COACHING MENTAL TOUGHNESS/CRITICAL THINKING FOR A LIVING"

The Mental Toughness University Licensee Program offers the unique opportunity to build your business on a foundation of world-class success. If you think you have what it takes to become a successful Mental Toughness Coach, email dawn@govesiebold.com or call 561.733.9078 to receive a no obligation application.

"Becoming a Mental Toughness University Licensee is one the best business decisions I've ever made. I earned $212,000 working part time in the first 18 months"

– Dr. Alok Trivedi, Chicago, Illinois

Mental Toughness for Dieters

Register for this FREE 21-day video coaching course and lose weight now!

Each day for the next 21 days you'll receive an email with a link to your 10-15 minute training video for the day. After you watch the video answer three short questions about how you're feeling about your progress. After 21-days of Mental Toughness Training for weight loss, you'll have the tools you need to go the distance and create the body you desire and deserve. Watch the introduction video above, register for the FREE course and get started now! Your new body and your new life are waiting!

visit www.fatloser.com

Are you interested in building a million-dollar speaking career?

Course Details

This 10-day course is designed to give you an insider's overview of the professional speaking business and teach you how to build a million-dollar speaking career. Over the course of 10-days, you'll have access to one short 10-15 minute video per day, complete with questions to answer that will help you create a customized speaking business tailored to your expertise, interests, and financial goals.

You Will Learn...

- ✓ How to select your topic
- ✓ How to build a multi-dimensional business model
- ✓ How to become a personality speaker
- ✓ How to break into the two major speaking markets
- ✓ How to leverage the power of your keynote speech
- ✓ How to become a niche market celebrity
- ✓ How to build your referral network
- ✓ How to become a profitable author
- ✓ How to sell yourself as a professional speaker
    ...And much more

Each day you will watch a short video and answer homework questions. Upon successful completion of this course, you will receive an official certificate of achievement. As a graduate, you will know more about the inner-workings of the professional speaking business than most professional speakers. No kidding. Here's why: Your coach for the 10-day course is Steve Siebold, CSP. Steve Siebold ranks among the top 1% of income earners worldwide in the professional speaking industry. Siebold was the protégé of the late Bill Gove, the father of the professional speaking industry, and one of the most successful keynote speakers of all-time. After attending the Bill Gove Speech Workshop in 1996, and spending five years on the road speaking with Mr. Gove, Steve Siebold rocketed to the top tier of the speaking industry and became a million-dollar professional speaker. Steve Siebold will give you insights into the speaking business that only a handful of speakers in the business fully understand, and how you can use them to live your dreams as a fee-paid professional speaker.

You get all of this for FREE. No catch. No strings. Your new career is waiting for you.

Register at www.FreeSpeakingcourse.com today!

The Video Blog based on the best-selling book hosted by author Steve Siebold. Every week the SPR blog tackles a controversial topic or hot button issue and challenges SPR fans around the world to sound off and state their opinions.

Subscribers include executives, entrepreneurs, politicians, college professors, journalists, thought leaders and concerned citizens worldwide.

All we're missing is YOU!

Get your FREE SUBSCRIPTION at

www.SexPoliticsReligionBlog.com

SEX ★ POLITICS ★ RELIGION RADIO SHOW

Wednesday's — 2-3 pm Eastern

This weekly radio show is hosted by Steve Siebold and includes over 100 guest/expert correspondents.

Every Wednesday from 2 pm-3 pm the SPR Radio Show takes on America's most pressing issues with special guests and live caller interaction. This is one of the most entertaining programs you'll ever hear.

Listen is as tempers flare, emotions soar and arguments ensue as passionate parties from both sides of the political, social and religious spectrum engage in respectful discourse.

SPR Radio Show Topics Include:

Sex ★ Open Marriage ★ War on Drugs

Obama Care ★ Organized Religion ★ The Bible

Prostitution ★ Pornography ★ Gun Control

Assisted Suicide ★ God ★ The Church

Pre-Marital Sex ★ Gay Marriage ★ Death Penalty

School Bullying ★ Evolution ★ School Prayer

And many more of the controversial issues of our time!

Subscribe Today and Listen In!
www.blogtalkradio.com/sexpoliticsreligion

ABOUT THE AUTHOR

Steve Siebold is a former professional athlete and national coach. He's spent the past 28 years studying the thought processes, habits and philosophies of world class performers. Today he helps Fortune 500 companies increase sales through mental toughness training and critical thinking processes. His clients include Johnson & Johnson, Toyota, and Procter & Gamble. He's written five books on mental toughness with over 200,000 copies in print. He's appeared on The Today Show, Good Morning America, ABC News and dozens of other TV shows around the world. He's quoted regularly in the Wall Street Journal, Fortune, Forbes and numerous other business publications. Steve was named the 2011 Chairman of the National Speakers Associations Million Dollar Speakers Group, which consists of 39 of the wealthiest professional speakers in the world. His numerous television appearances can be seen at www.SteveOnTV.com